D0015464

Julius Caesar

and Related Readings

McDougal Littell
A HOUGHTON MIFFLIN COMPANY
Evanston, Illinois   *Boston*   *Dallas*

Acknowledgments

Carcanet Press: Excerpt from "Julius Caesar" from *The Twelve Caesars* by Suetonius, translated by Robert Graves; Copyright 1957 by Robert Graves. Reprinted by permission of Carcanet Press Ltd.

Random House, Inc: "Epitaph on a Tyrant" from *W. H. Auden: Collected Poems* by W. H. Auden; Copyright 1940 and renewed © 1968 by W. H. Auden. Reprinted by permission of Random House, Inc.

The New York Times: "Kennedy Is Killed by Sniper . . ." by Tom Wicker from *The New York Times*, November 23, 1963. Copyright © 1963 by The New York Times Company. Reprinted by permission of The New York Times.

The Rod Serling Trust: *Back There* by Rod Serling. Copyright © 1960 by Rod Serling, renewed © 1988 by Carolyn Serling, Jodi Serling, and Anne Serling. All rights reserved.

Broadside Press: "For Malcolm, a Year After" from *Poems from Prison* by Etheridge Knight. Reprinted by permission of Broadside Press.

Time Inc.: "The Agony of Victory" by William Oscar Johnson, special reporting by Lester Munson, from *Sports Illustrated*, July 5, 1993; Copyright © 1993 by Time Inc. All rights reserved. Reprinted courtesy of Sports Illustrated, a division of Time Inc.

James Thurber Literary Properties: "The Tiger Who Would Be King" from *Further Fables for Our Times* by James Thurber. Copyright 1956 by James Thurber, renewed © 1984 by Rosemary A. Thurber. Reprinted by permission of James Thurber Literary Properties.

Cover illustration by John Patrick.
Author photo: North Wind Picture Archive.

ISBN 0-395-77542-6

234567—DCI—02 01 00 99 98 97 96

Contents

Continued

Julius Caesar

William Shakespeare

Characters

Julius Caesar

TRIUMVIRS AFTER THE DEATH OF JULIUS CAESAR

Octavius Caesar

Marcus Antonius

M. Aemilius Lepidus

SENATORS

Cicero

Publius

Popilius Lena

CONSPIRATORS AGAINST JULIUS CAESAR

Marcus Brutus

Cassius

Casca

Trebonius

Ligarius

Decius Brutus

Metellus Cimber

Cinna

Flavius and Marullus, Tribunes of the people

Artemidorus of Cnidos, a teacher of Rhetoric

A Soothsayer

Cinna, a poet

Another Poet

FRIENDS TO BRUTUS AND CASSIUS

Lucilius

Titinius

Messala

Young Cato

Volumnius

SERVANTS TO BRUTUS

Varro

Clitus

Claudius

Strato

Lucius

Dardanius

Pindarus, servant to Cassius

Calpurnia, wife to Caesar

Portia, wife to Brutus

The Ghost of Caesar

Senators, Citizens, Guards, Attendants, Servants, etc.

Time: 44 B.C.

Place: Rome; the camp near Sardis; the plains of Philippi

3-6 ***What, know . . . profession:*** Since you are workers
(mechanical), you should be carrying the tools of your
trade *(sign / Of your profession).* What is Flavius'
attitude toward these workers?

11-31 In this conversation, the *cobbler* (shoemaker) makes
several puns, which all go over the head of Marullus.
Imagine the workmen laughing, as Marullus gets
angrier and angrier, wondering what's so funny.

ACT ONE

Scene 1 *A street in Rome.*

*The play begins on February 15, the religious
feast of Lupercal. Today the people have a
particular reason for celebrating. Julius Caesar
has just returned to Rome after a long civil
war in which he defeated the forces of
Pompey, his rival for power. Caesar now has
the opportunity to take full control of Rome.*

*In this opening scene, a group of workmen, in
their best clothes, celebrate in the streets.
They are joyful over Caesar's victory. The
workers meet Flavius and Marullus, two
tribunes—government officials—who
supported Pompey. The tribunes express their
anger at the celebration, and one worker
responds with puns. Finally, the two tribunes
scatter the crowd.*

Flavius. Hence! home, you idle creatures, get you
    home!
  Is this a holiday? What, know you not,
  Being mechanical, you ought not walk
5   Upon a laboring day without the sign
  Of your profession? Speak, what trade art thou?

First Commoner. Why, sir, a carpenter.

Marullus. Where is thy leather apron and thy rule?
  What dost thou with thy best apparel on? You, sir,
10   what trade are you?

Second Commoner. Truly sir, in respect of a fine
  workman I am but, as you would say, a cobbler.

18-19 Marullus accuses the commoner of being a wicked, sly person *(naughty knave)*, but the commoner begs Marullus not to be angry with him *(be not out with me)*.

22-23 Marullus thinks the cobbler means "I can mend your behavior." He accuses the cobbler of being disrespectful *(saucy)*.

26 The cobbler jokes about the similarity of *awl* (a shoemaker's tool) to the word *all. Do you or any of your friends ever make up puns?*

31 *neat's leather:* calfskin, used to make expensive shoes. The cobbler means that even rich people come to him for shoes.

32 *wherefore:* why.

40-41 *What . . . wheels:* What captured prisoners march chained to the wheels of his chariot?

45 *Pompey:* a former Roman ruler defeated by Caesar in 48 B.C. Pompey was murdered a year after his defeat.

Marullus. But what trade art thou? Answer me directly.

15 **Second Commoner.** A trade, sir, that I hope I may use with a safe conscience, which is indeed, sir, a mender of bad soles.

Marullus. What trade, thou knave? Thou naughty knave, what trade?

20 **Second Commoner.** Nay, I beseech you, sir, be not out with me. Yet if you be out, sir, I can mend you.

Marullus. What mean'st thou by that? Mend me, thou saucy fellow?

Second Commoner. Why, sir, cobble you.

25 **Flavius.** Thou art a cobbler, art thou?

Second Commoner. Truly, sir, all that I live by is with the awl. I meddle with no tradesman's matters nor women's matters, but with all. I am indeed, sir, a surgeon to old shoes. When they are in great
30 danger, I recover them. As proper men as ever trod upon neat's leather have gone upon my handiwork.

Flavius. But wherefore art not in thy shop today? Why dost thou lead these men about the streets?

Second Commoner. Truly, sir, to wear out their shoes,
35 to get myself into more work. But indeed, sir, we make holiday to see Caesar and to rejoice in his triumph.

Marullus. Wherefore rejoice? What conquest brings he home?
40 What tributaries follow him to Rome
To grace in captive bonds his chariot wheels?
You blocks, you stones, you worse than senseless things!
O you hard hearts, you cruel men of Rome!
45 Knew you not Pompey? Many a time and oft

53 **Tiber:** a river that runs through Rome.

54 **replication:** echo.

57 **cull out:** select.

59 **Pompey's blood:** Caesar is returning to Rome in triumph after defeating Pompey's sons in Spain.

62-63 **intermit . . . ingratitude:** hold back the deadly illness that might be just punishment for your behavior.

66-68 **weep . . . of all:** Weep into the Tiber River until it overflows.

Exeunt *(Latin):* They leave.

69 Flavius and Marullus are now alone, having shamed the workers into leaving the street. Flavius says that they will now see if they have touched **(moved)** the workers' poor characters **(basest metal).**

72-73 **Disrobe . . . ceremonies:** Strip the statues of any decorations you find on them.

77-79 **I'll about . . . thick:** I'll go around and scatter the rest of the commoners. Do the same yourself wherever they are forming a crowd.

Have you climbed up to walls and battlements,
To tow'rs and windows, yea, to chimney tops,
Your infants in your arms, and there have sat
The livelong day, with patient expectation,
50 To see great Pompey pass the streets of Rome.
And when you saw his chariot but appear,
Have you not made an universal shout,
That Tiber trembled underneath her banks
To hear the replication of your sounds
55 Made in her concave shores?
And do you now put on your best attire?
And do you now cull out a holiday?
And do you now strew flowers in his way
That comes in triumph over Pompey's blood?
60 Be gone!
Run to your houses, fall upon your knees,
Pray to the gods to intermit the plague
That needs must light on this ingratitude.

Flavius. Go, go, good countrymen, and for this fault
65 Assemble all the poor men of your sort;
Draw them to Tiber banks, and weep your tears
Into the channel, till the lowest stream
Do kiss the most exalted shores of all.

[Exeunt all the Commoners.*]*

See, whe'r their basest metal be not moved.
70 They vanish tongue-tied in their guiltiness.
Go you down that way towards the Capitol;
This way will I. Disrobe the images
If you do find them decked with ceremonies.

Marullus. May we do so?
75 You know it is the feast of Lupercal.

Flavius. It is no matter. Let no images
Be hung with Caesar's trophies. I'll about
And drive away the vulgar from the streets
So do you too, where you perceive them thick.

80-83 ***These . . . fearfulness:*** Flavius compares Caesar to a
  bird. He hopes that turning away some of Caesar's
  supporters **(growing feathers)** will prevent him from
  becoming too powerful.

5-11 ***Stand . . . curse:*** Antony **(Antonius)** is about to run
  in a race that is part of the Lupercal celebration.
  Caesar refers to the superstition that a **sterile** woman
  (one unable to bear children) can become fertile if
  touched by one of the racers.

80   These growing feathers plucked from Caesar's wing
      Will make him fly an ordinary pitch,
      Who else would soar above the view of men
      And keep us all in servile fearfulness.

[Exeunt.]

Scene 2 *A public place in Rome.*

*As Caesar attends the traditional race at the
festival of Lupercal, a soothsayer warns him to
beware of the ides of March, or March 15. (The
middle day of each month was called the ides.)
When Caesar leaves, Cassius and Brutus speak.
Cassius tries to turn Brutus against Caesar by
using flattery, examples of Caesar's weaknesses,
and sarcasm about Caesar's power. Caesar
passes by again, expressing his distrust of
Cassius. Cassius and Brutus learn of Caesar's
rejection of a crown the people of Rome have
offered him. They agree to meet again to
discuss what must be done about Caesar.*

[A flourish of trumpets announces the approach of Caesar.
A large crowd of Commoners *has assembled; a*
Soothsayer *is among them. Enter* Caesar, *his wife,*
Calpurnia, Portia, Decius, Cicero, Brutus, Cassius, Casca,
and Antony, *who is stripped for running in the games.]*

Caesar. Calpurnia.

Casca.   Peace, ho! Caesar speaks.

Caesar.   Calpurnia.

Calpurnia. Here, my lord.

5 **Caesar.** Stand you directly in Antonius' way
    When he doth run his course. Antonius.

Antonius. Caesar, my lord?

Caesar. Forget not in your speed, Antonius,

12-13 *I shall . . . performed:* What do these lines tell you about Antony's attitude toward Caesar?

15-17 Remember that the crowd is cheering constantly. The **soothsayer** (fortuneteller), who calls out Caesar's name can hardly be heard. Casca tells the crowd to quiet down.

18 *press:* crowd

21 *ides:* the middle day of the month.

30-33 Cassius asks if Brutus is going to watch the race *(the order of the course),* but Brutus says he is not fond of sports *(gamesome).*

To touch Calpurnia; for our elders say
10 The barren, touched in this holy chase,
Shake off their sterile curse.

Antonius.   I shall remember.
When Caesar says "Do this," it is performed.

Caesar. Set on, and leave no ceremony out.

[Flourish of trumpets. Caesar starts to leave.]

15 **Soothsayer.** Caesar!

Caesar. Ha! Who calls?

Casca. Bid every noise be still. Peace yet again?

Caesar. Who is it in the press that calls on me?
I hear a tongue shriller than all the music
20 Cry "Caesar!" Speak. Caesar is turned to hear.

Soothsayer. Beware the ides of March.

Caesar.   What man is that?

Brutus. A soothsayer bids you beware the ides of March.

Caesar. Set him before me; let me see his face.

25 **Cassius.** Fellow, come from the throng; look upon
Caesar.

Caesar. What say'st thou to me now? Speak once again.

Soothsayer. Beware the ides of March.

Caesar. He is a dreamer; let us leave him. Pass.

[Trumpets sound. Exeunt all but Brutus and Cassius.]

30 **Cassius.** Will you go see the order of the course?

Brutus. Not I.

Cassius. I pray you do.

Brutus. I am not gamesome. I do lack some part
Of that quick spirit that is in Antony.

37-39 *I do observe . . . to have:* Lately I haven't seen the
friendliness in your face that I used to see *(was wont
to have).* *Can you sometimes look into a friend's eyes
and tell how he or she is feeling?*

44-53 *I turn . . . other men:* I have been frowning at myself,
not at you. I have been troubled *(Vexed)* lately by
mixed emotions *(passions of some difference).* They
are personal matters that are, perhaps, marring my
good manners. I hope my friends won't interpret
(construe) my actions as anything more than my own
private concerns. *Do you ever avoid your friends when
you have a lot on your mind?*

54-57 *I have . . . cogitations:* I have misunderstood your
feelings. As a result, I have kept certain thoughts to
myself.

62-69 *it is . . . eyes:* It is too bad you don't have a mirror
that would show you your inner qualities *(hidden
worthiness).* In fact, many respected citizens suffering
under Caesar's rule *(this age's yoke)* have wished that
Brutus could see how much better he is than Caesar.
What is Cassius trying to tell Brutus?

35   Let me not hinder, Cassius, your desires.
    I'll leave you.

Cassius. Brutus, I do observe you now of late;
    I have not from your eyes that gentleness
    And show of love as I was wont to have.
40   You bear too stubborn and too strange a hand
    Over your friend that loves you.

Brutus.   Cassius,
    Be not deceived. If I have veiled my look,
    I turn the trouble of my countenance
45   Merely upon myself. Vexed I am
    Of late with passions of some difference,
    Conceptions only proper to myself,
    Which give some soil, perhaps, to my behaviors;
    But let not therefore my good friends be grieved
50   (Among which number, Cassius, be you one)
    Nor construe any further my neglect
    Than that poor Brutus, with himself at war,
    forgets the shows of love to other men.

Cassius. Then, Brutus, I have much mistook your
55   passion,
    By means whereof this breast of mine hath buried
    Thoughts of great value, worthy cogitations.
    Tell me, good Brutus, can you see your face?

Brutus. No, Cassius, for the eye sees not itself
60   But by reflection, by some other things.

Cassius. 'Tis just.
    And it is very much lamented, Brutus,
    That you have no such mirrors as will turn
    Your hidden worthiness into your eye,
65   That you might see your shadow. I have heard
    Where many of the best respect in Rome
    (Except immortal Caesar), speaking of Brutus
    And groaning underneath this age's yoke,
    Have wished that noble Brutus had his eyes.

73-77 **_Therefore . . . not of:_** Listen, Brutus, since you cannot see yourself, I will be your mirror **_(glass)_** and show you what you truly are.

78 **_jealous on me:_** suspicious of me.

79-85 **_Were I . . . dangerous:_** If you think I am a fool **_(common laugher)_** or someone who pretends to be the friend of everyone I meet; or if you believe that I show friendship and then talk evil about my friends **_(scandal them)_** behind their backs, or that I try to win the affections of the common people **_(all the rout)_**, then consider me dangerous and don't trust me.

88-89 **_do you . . . it so:_** Imagine Cassius blurting out this line, maybe a little more eagerly than he had intended. He is trying to find a meaning in Brutus' words that may or may not be there.

93-95 **_If it . . . indifferently:_** If what you have in mind concerns the good of Rome **_(the general good)_**, I would face either honor or death to do what must be done.

99 **_outward favor:_** physical appearance.

103-104 **_I had . . . I myself:_** I would rather not live, than to live in awe of someone no better than I am.

70 **Brutus.** Into what dangers would you lead me, Cassius,
That you would have me seek into myself
For that which is not in me?

   Cassius. Therefore, good Brutus, be prepared to hear;
And since you know you cannot see yourself
75 So well as by reflection, I, your glass,
Will modestly discover to yourself
That of yourself which you yet know not of.
And be not jealous on me, gentle Brutus.
Were I a common laugher, or did use
80 To stale with ordinary oaths my love
To every new protester; if you know
That I do fawn on men and hug them hard,
And after scandal them; or if you know
That I profess myself in banqueting
85 To all the rout, then hold me dangerous.

   [Flourish and shout.]

   Brutus. What means this shouting? I do fear the people
Choose Caesar for their king.

   Cassius.   Ay, do you fear it?
Then must I think you would not have it so.

90 **Brutus.** I would not, Cassius, yet I love him well.
But wherefore do you hold me here so long?
What is it that you would impart to me?
If it be aught toward the general good,
Set honor in one eye and death i' the other,
95 And I will look on both indifferently;
For let the gods so speed me as I love
The name of honor more than I fear death.

   Cassius. I know that virtue to be in you, Brutus,
As well as I do know your outward favor.
100 Well, honor is the subject of my story.
I cannot tell what you and other men
Think of this life, but for my single self,
I had as lief not be as live to be

109 ***troubled . . . shores:*** The Tiber River was rising in the middle of a storm.

113 ***Accoutered:*** dressed.

115-117 ***we did . . . controversy:*** We fought the tide with strong muscles ***(lusty sinews)***, conquering it with our spirit of competition ***(hearts of controversy)***.

118 ***ere:*** before.

120-123 ***I, as Aeneas . . . Caesar:*** Aeneas (in nē′ es), the mythological founder of Rome, carried his father, Anchises (an kī′ sēz), out of the burning city of Troy. Cassius says he did the same for Caesar when Caesar could no longer swim in the raging river.

125 ***bend his body:*** bow.

130 ***His coward . . . fly:*** His lips turned pale.

131 ***bend:*** glance.

133-139 ***that tongue . . . alone:*** The same tongue that has led Romans to memorize his speeches cried out in the tone of a sick girl. I'm amazed that such a weak man should get ahead of the rest of the world and appear as the victor ***(bear the palm)*** all by himself. (A palm leaf was a symbol of victory in war.)

In awe of such a thing as I myself.
105 I was born free as Caesar, so were you;
We both have fed as well, and we can both
Endure the winter's cold as well as he.
For once, upon a raw and gusty day,
The troubled Tiber chafing with her shores,
110 Caesar said to me, "Dar'st thou, Cassius, now
Leap in with me into this angry flood
And swim to yonder point?" Upon the word,
Accoutered as I was, I plunged in
And bade him follow. So indeed he did.
115 The torrent roared, and we did buffet it
With lusty sinews, throwing it aside
And stemming it with hearts of controversy.
But ere we could arrive the point proposed,
Caesar cried, "Help me, Cassius, or I sink!"
120 I, as Aeneas, our great ancestor,
Did from the flames of Troy upon his shoulder
The old Anchises bear, so from the waves of Tiber
Did I the tired Caesar. And this man
Is now become a god, and Cassius is
125 A wretched creature and must bend his body
If Caesar carelessly but nod on him.
He had a fever when he was in Spain,
And when the fit was on him, I did mark
How he did shake. 'Tis true, this god did shake.
130 His coward lips did from their color fly,
And that same eye whose bend doth awe the world
Did lose his luster. I did hear him groan.
Ay, and that tongue of his that bade the Romans
Mark him and write his speeches in their books,
135 Alas, it cried, "Give me some drink, Titinius,"
As a sick girl! Ye gods! it doth amaze me
A man of such a feeble temper should
So get the start of the majestic world
And bear the palm alone.

[Shout. Flourish.]

140-142 **Another . . . on Caesar:** The shouts of the crowd are coming from offstage. Brutus is troubled by this cheering for Caesar, worried about where it might lead.

143-145 **he doth . . . Colossus:** Cassius compares Caesar to Colossus, the huge statue of the Greek god Apollo at Rhodes. The statue supposedly spanned the entrance to the harbor and was so high that ships could sail through the space between its legs. *What is Cassius' tone in these lines?*

149-150 **The fault . . . underlings:** It is not the stars that have determined our fate; we are inferiors through our own fault.

156 **Conjure:** call up spirits.

160 **Age . . . shamed:** It is a shameful time *(Age)* in which to be living.

169-171 **There was . . . a king:** Cassius is referring to an ancestor of Brutus who drove invading kings from Rome.

172 **am nothing jealous:** am sure.

173 **have some aim:** can guess.

174-177 **How I have . . . moved:** I will tell you later *(recount hereafter)* my thoughts about this topic. For now, I ask you as a friend not to try to convince me further.

140 **Brutus.** Another general shout?
I do believe that these applauses are
For some new honors that are heaped on Caesar.

Cassius. Why, man, he doth bestride the narrow
world
145 Like a Colossus, and we petty men
Walk under his huge legs and peep about
To find ourselves dishonorable graves.
Men at some time are masters of their fates.
The fault, dear Brutus, is not in our stars,
150 But in ourselves, that we are underlings.
"Brutus," and "Caesar." What should be in that
"Caesar?"
Why should that name be sounded more than yours?
Write them together: yours is as fair a name.
155 Sound them, it doth become the mouth as well.
Weigh them, it is as heavy. Conjure with 'em:
"Brutus" will start a spirit as soon as "Caesar."
Now in the names of all the gods at once,
Upon what meat doth this our Caesar feed
160 That he is grown so great? Age, thou are shamed!
Rome, thou hast lost the breed of noble bloods!
When went there by an age since the great Flood
But it was famed with more than with one man?
When could they say (till now) that talked of Rome
165 That her wide walls encompassed but one man?
Now is it Rome indeed, and room enough,
When there is in it but one only man!
O, you and I have heard our fathers say
There was a Brutus once that would have brooked
170 The eternal devil to keep his state in Rome
As easily as a king.

Brutus. That you do love me I am nothing jealous.
What you would work me to, I have some aim.
How I have thought of this, and of these times,
175 I shall recount hereafter. For this present,
I would not (so with love I might entreat you)

180 *meet:* appropriate.

183 *repute himself:* present himself as.

185 *What do you think Brutus might be prepared to do?*

190 The private conversation is now over. Caesar and his admirers return, with the crowd following close behind.

193 *worthy note:* worth remembering.

196 *chidden train:* a group of followers who have been scolded.

197-200 *Cicero . . . senators:* Cicero was a highly respected senator. Brutus says he has the angry look of a **ferret** (a fierce little animal), the look he gets when other senators disagree with him at the Capitol.

202-226 Brutus and Cassius take Casca aside. The conversation Caesar has with Antony is not heard by any of the other characters around them.

Be any further moved. What you have said
I will consider; what you have to say
I will with patience hear, and find a time
180   Both meet to hear and answer such high things.
Till then, my noble friend, chew upon this:
Brutus had rather be a villager
Than to repute himself a son of Rome
Under these hard conditions as this time
185   Is like to lay upon us.

Cassius.   I am glad
That my weak words have struck but thus much
show
Of fire from Brutus.

[Voices and Music are heard approaching.]

190   **Brutus.** The games are done, and Caesar is returning.

Cassius. As they pass by, pluck Casca by the sleeve,
And he will (after his sour fashion) tell you
What hath proceeded worthy note today.

[Reenter Caesar and his train of followers.]

Brutus. I will do so. But look you, Cassius!
195   The angry spot doth glow on Caesar's brow,
And all the rest look like a chidden train.
Calpurnia's cheek is pale, and Cicero
Looks with such ferret and such fiery eyes
As we have seen him in the Capitol,
200   Being crossed in conference by some senators.

Cassius. Casca will tell us what the matter is.

[Caesar looks at Cassius and turns to Antony.]

Caesar. Antonius.

Antonius. Caesar?

Caesar. Let me have men about me that are fat,
205   Sleek-headed men, and such as sleep o' nights.

209 ***well given:*** Antony says that Cassius, despite his appearance, is a supporter of Caeser.

212-215 ***I do not . . . of men:*** Caesar labels Cassius dangerous and, at the same time, one who can see through people and understand their secrets. Caesar makes a boast about himself. *What does he boast of?*

222 *What is Caesar's opinion of Cassius? Why does he feel this way?*

225 *What does Caesar reveal about himself in this line?*

227 Now only Brutus, Cassius, and Casca remain on stage.

229 ***hath chanced:*** has happened.

235 ***put it by:*** pushed it aside.

Yond Cassius has a lean and hungry look;
He thinks too much, such men are dangerous.

Antonius. Fear him not, Caesar, he's not dangerous.
He is a noble Roman, and well given.

210 **Caesar.** Would he were fatter! But I fear him not.
Yet if my name were liable to fear,
I do not know the man I should avoid
So soon as that spare Cassius. He reads much,
He is a great observer, and he looks
215 Quite through the deeds of men. He loves no plays
As thou dost, Antony; he hears no music.
Seldom he smiles, and smiles in such a sort
As if he mocked himself and scorned his spirit
That could be moved to smile at anything.
220 Such men as he be never at heart's ease
Whiles they behold a greater than themselves,
And therefore are they very dangerous.
I rather tell thee what is to be feared
Than what I fear, for always I am Caesar.
225 Come on my right hand, for this ear is deaf,
And tell me truly what thou think'st of him.

[Trumpets sound. Exeunt Caesar *and all his train except*
Casca, *who stays behind.]*

Casca. You pulled me by the cloak. Would you speak
with me?

Brutus. Ay, Casca. Tell us what hath chanced today
230 That Caesar looks so sad.

Casca. Why, you were with him, were you not?

Brutus. I should not then ask Casca what had
chanced.

Casca. Why, there was a crown offered him; and
235 being offered him, he put it by with the back of his
hand, thus. And then the people fell a-shouting.

243 **_Ay, marry, was't:_** Yes, indeed, it was. _Marry_ was a mild oath used in Shakespeare's time (but not in ancient Rome). The word means "by the Virgin Mary."

252 **_coronets:_** small crowns made out of laurel branches twisted together. A coronet was less of an honor than the kind of crown a king would wear.

254 **_fain:_** gladly.

256 **_loath:_** reluctant.

258-259 **_rabblement:_** unruly crowd.

263 **_swounded:_** fainted.

266 **_soft:_** Wait a moment.

268-270 There is some historical evidence that Caesar had epilepsy. In Shakespeare's time, this illness was known as the falling sickness (because someone having an epileptic seizure is likely to fall to the floor).

Brutus. What was the second noise for?

Casca. Why, for that too.

Cassius. They shouted thrice. What was the last cry
240   for?

Casca. Why, for that too.

Brutus. Was the crown offered him thrice?

Casca. Ay, marry, was't! and he put it by thrice, every
time gentler than other; and at every putting-by
245   mine honest neighbors shouted.

Cassius. Who offered him the crown?

Casca. Why, Antony.

Brutus. Tell us the manner of it, gentle Casca.

Casca. I can as well be hanged as tell the manner of it.
250   It was mere foolery; I did not mark it. I saw Mark
Antony offer him a crown—yet 'twas not a crown
neither, 'twas one of these coronets—and, as I told
you, he put it by once. But for all that, to my
thinking, he would fain have had it. Then he offered
255   it to him again; then he put it by again; but to my
thinking, he was very loath to lay his fingers off it.
And then he offered it the third time. He put it the
third time by; and still as he refused it, the rabble-
ment hooted, and clapped their chapped hands, and
260   threw up their sweaty nightcaps, and uttered such
a deal of stinking breath because Caesar refused the
crown that it had, almost, choked Caesar; for he
swounded and fell down at it. And for mine own
part, I durst not laugh, for fear of opening my lips
265   and receiving the bad air.

Cassius. But soft, I pray you. What, did Caesar
swound?

Casca. He fell down in the market place and foamed

272 Cassius sarcastically uses the phrase *falling sickness* to refer to the tendency to bow down before Caesar.

281 *ope his doublet:* open his jacket.

282-284 *An . . . rogues:* If *(An)* I had been a worker with a proper tool, may I go to hell with the sinners *(rogues)* if I would not have done as he asked *(taken him at a word)*.

286 *amiss:* wrong.

287 *infirmity:* sickness.

288 *wenches:* common women.

at mouth and was speechless.

270 **Brutus.** 'Tis very like. He hath the falling sickness.

Cassius. No, Caesar hath not it; but you, and I, and honest Casca, we have the falling sickness.

Casca. I know not what you mean by that, but I am sure Caesar fell down. If the tag-rag people did not
275 clap him and hiss him, according as he pleased and displeased them, as they use to do the players in the theater, I am no true man.

Brutus. What said he when he came unto himself?

Casca. Marry, before he fell down, when he perceived
280 the common herd was glad he refused the crown, he plucked me ope his doublet and offered them his throat to cut. An I had been a man of any occupation, if I would not have taken him at a word I would I might go to hell among the rogues. And so
285 he fell. When he came to himself again, he said, if he had done or said anything amiss, he desired their worships to think it was his infirmity. Three or four wenches where I stood cried, "Alas, good soul!" and forgave him with all their hearts. But there's no heed
290 to be taken of them. If Caesar had stabbed their mothers, they would have done no less.

Brutus. And after that, he came thus sad away?

Casca. Ay.

Cassius. Did Cicero say anything?

295 **Casca.** Ay, he spoke Greek.

Cassius. To what effect?

Casca. Nay, an I tell you that, I'll ne'er look you i' the face again. But those that understood him smiled at one another and shook their heads; but for mine
300 own part, it was Greek to me. I could tell you more

302 *put to silence:* This may mean that the two tribunes have been put to death or that they have been barred from public life.

305 *I am promised forth:* I have another appointment.

312 *quick mettle:* clever, intelligent.

313-318 *So is . . . appetite:* Cassius says that Casca can still be intelligent in carrying out an important project. He only pretends to be slow *(tardy).* His rude manner makes people more willing to accept *(digest)* the things he says.

324-338 Now Cassius is alone on stage. The thoughts he expresses in this speech are thoughts he would not want Brutus to know about.

325-326 *Thy . . . disposed:* Your honorable nature can be manipulated *(wrought)* into something not quite so honorable.

329 *bear me hard:* hold a grudge against me.

news, too. Marullus and Flavius, for pulling scarfs
off Caesar's images, are put to silence. Fare you well.
There was more foolery yet, if I could remember it.

Cassius. Will you sup with me tonight, Casca?

305 **Casca.** No, I am promised forth.

Cassius. Will you dine with me tomorrow?

Casca. Ay, if I be alive, and your mind hold, and your
dinner worth eating.

Cassius. Good. I will expect you.

310 **Casca.** Do so. Farewell both.

[Exit.]

Brutus. What a blunt fellow is this grown to be!
He was quick mettle when he went to school.

Cassius. So is he now in execution
Of any bold or noble enterprise,
315 However he puts on this tardy form.
This rudeness is a sauce to his good wit,
Which gives men stomach to digest his words
With better appetite.

Brutus. And so it is. For this time I will leave you.
320 Tomorrow, if you please to speak with me,
I will come home to you; or if you will,
Come home to me, and I will wait for you.

Cassius. I will do so. Till then, think of the world.

[Exit Brutus.]

Well, Brutus, thou art noble; yet I see
325 Thy honorable mettle may be wrought
From that it is disposed. Therefore it is meet
That noble minds keep ever with their likes;
For who so firm that cannot be seduced?
Caesar doth bear me hard, but he loves Brutus.
330 If I were Brutus now and he were Cassius,

331 *He should . . . me:* I wouldn't let him get away with fooling me.

331-335 *I will . . . his name:* Cassius plans to leave messages at Brutus' home that appear to be from several people.

338 *we will . . . endure:* We will remove Caesar from his high position or suffer the consequences.

3 *sway of earth:* the natural order of things.

5 *tempests:* storms.

6 *rived:* torn.

8 *To be exalted with:* to raise themselves to the level of.

11-13 *Either . . . destruction:* Such a terrible storm could be caused by only two things—a civil war *(strife)* in heaven or angry gods destroying the world.

He should not humor me. I will this night,
In several hands, in at his windows throw,
As if they came from several citizens,
Writing, all tending to the great opinion
335 That Rome holds of his name; wherein obscurely
Caesar's ambition shall be glanced at.
And after this let Caesar seat him sure,
For we will shake him, or worse days endure.

[Exit.]

Scene 3 *A street in Rome.*

*It is the night of March 14. Amid violent
thunder and lightning, a terrified Casca fears
that the storm and other omens predict
terrible events to come. Cassius interprets the
storm as a sign that Caesar must be
overthrown. Cassius and Casca agree that
Caesar's rise to power must be stopped by any
means. Cinna, another plotter, enters, and
they discuss how to persuade Brutus to follow
their plan.*

*[Thunder and lightning. Enter, from opposite sides, Casca,
with his sword drawn, and Cicero.]*

Cicero. Good even, Casca. Brought you Caesar home?
Why are you breathless? and why stare you so?

Casca. Are not you moved when all the sway of earth
Shakes like a thing unfirm? O Cicero,
5 I have seen tempests when the scolding winds
Have rived the knotty oaks, and I have seen
The ambitious ocean swell and rage and foam
To be exalted with the threat'ning clouds;
But never till tonight, never till now,
10 Did I go through a tempest dropping fire.
Either there is a civil strife in heaven,
Or else the world, too saucy with the gods,

14 *saw . . . wonderful:* Did you see anything else that was strange?

19 *Not sensible of fire:* not feeling the fire.

20-21 *I ha' not . . . lion:* I haven't put my sword back into its scabbard since I saw a lion at the Capitol building.

23 *drawn / Upon:* huddled together.

27 *bird of night:* the owl, usually seen only at night.

29-33 *When these . . . upon:* When strange events *(prodigies)* like these happen at the same time *(conjointly meet),* no one should say there are natural explanations for them. I believe they are bad omens *(portentous things)* for the place where they happen.

34-36 *Indeed . . . themselves:* Cicero does not accept Casca's superstitious explanation of events. He agrees that the times are strange. But he says people can interpret events the way they want to, no matter what actually causes the events.

43 *Who's there:* Cassius probably has his sword out. Remember, with no light other than moonlight, it could be dangerous to come upon a stranger in the street.

Incenses them to send destruction.

Cicero. Why, saw you anything more wonderful?

15 **Casca.** A common slave—you know him well by
    sight—
  Held up his left hand, which did flame and burn
  Like twenty torches joined; and yet his hand,
  Not sensible of fire, remained unscorched.
20 Besides—I ha' not since put up my sword—
  Against the Capitol I met a lion,
  Who glared upon me, and went surly by
  Without annoying me. And there were drawn
  Upon a heap a hundred ghastly women,
25 Transformed with their fear, who swore they saw
  Men, all in fire, walk up and down the streets.
  And yesterday the bird of night did sit
  Even at noonday upon the market place,
  Hooting and shrieking. When these prodigies
30 Do so conjointly meet, let not men say,
  "These are their reasons, they are natural,"
  For I believe they are portentous things
  Unto the climate that they point upon.

Cicero. Indeed it is a strange-disposed time.
35 But men may construe things after their fashion,
  Clean from the purpose of the things themselves.
  Comes Caesar to the Capitol tomorrow?

Casca. He doth, for he did bid Antonius
  Send word to you he would be there tomorrow.

40 **Cicero.** Good night then, Casca. This disturbed sky
  Is not to walk in.

Casca.   Farewell, Cicero.

[Exit Cicero.]

[Enter Cassius.]

Cassius. Who's there?

51-57 *For my . . . flash of it:* Cassius brags that he offered himself to the dangerous night, with his coat open *(unbraced),* exposing his chest to the thunder and lightning. *Why might he do this?*

60-62 *It is . . . astonish us:* Men are supposed to tremble when the gods use signs *(tokens)* to send frightening messengers *(heralds)* to scare us.

64 *want:* lack.

68-77 Cassius insists that heaven has brought about such things as birds and animals that change their natures *(from quality and kind),* children who predict the future *(calculate);* all these beings that act unnaturally *(change from their ordinance / Their natures, and preformed faculties).* Heaven has done all this, he says, to warn the Romans of an evil condition that they should correct.

Casca. A Roman.

45 **Cassius.** Casca, by your voice.

Casca. Your ear is good. Cassius, what night is this!

Cassius. A very pleasing night to honest men.

Casca. Who ever knew the heavens menace so?

Cassius. Those that have known the earth so full of
50   faults.
For my part, I have walked about the streets,
Submitting me unto the perilous night,
And, thus unbraced, Casca, as you see,
Have bared my bosom to the thunder-stone;
55 And when the cross blue lightning seemed to open
The breast of heaven, I did present myself
Even in the aim and very flash of it.

Casca. But wherefore did you so much tempt the
    heavens?
60 It is the part of men to fear and tremble
When the most mighty gods by tokens send
Such dreadful heralds to astonish us.

Cassius. You are dull, Casca, and those sparks of life
That should be in a Roman you do want,
65 Or else you use not. You look pale, and gaze,
And put on fear, and cast yourself in wonder,
To see the strange impatience of the heavens.
But if you would consider the true cause
Why all these fires, who all these gliding ghosts,
70 Why birds and beasts, from quality and kind;
Why old men fool and children calculate;
Why all these things change from their ordinance,
Their natures, and preformed faculties,
To monstrous quality, why, you shall find
75 That heaven hath infused them with these spirits
To make them instruments of fear and warning
Unto some monstrous state.

83 *prodigious grown:* become enormous and threatening. *To whom does Cassius refer in lines 76-82?*

86-90 *Romans . . . womanish:* Modern Romans have muscles *(thews)* and limbs like our ancestors, but we have the minds of our mothers, not our fathers. Our acceptance of a dictator *(yoke and sufferance)* shows us to be like women, not like men. (In Shakespeare's time—and in ancient Rome—women were considered weak creatures.)

93-94 *he shall . . . Italy:* The senators will make Caesar the king of all Roman territories except *(save)* Rome itself *(Italy),* since Romans would never let their own land be ruled by a king.

95-96 *I know . . . deliver Cassius:* I will free myself from slavery *(bondage)* by killing myself *(wear this dagger).*

97-103 Cassius shouts these lines toward the sky, trying to be heard over the thunder. Only through suicide, he says angrily, do the gods make the weak strong and able to defeat tyrants. The strong spirit cannot be imprisoned by tower, metal walls, dungeons, or iron chains. The reason is that one can always commit suicide *(life . . . Never lacks power to dismiss itself). Do you think Cassius would really kill himself?*

110-118 *And why . . . as Caesar:* Cassius goes into a tirade about Caesar, saying things for which he could be put to death. He says the only reason for Caesar's strength is the weakness of the Romans. They are *hinds* (female deer) and trash *(offal)* for allowing such a person as Caesar to come to power.

Now could I, Casca, name to thee a man
Most like this dreadful night
80 That thunders, lightens, opens graves, and roars
As doth the lion in the Capitol;
A man no mightier than thyself or me
In personal action, yet prodigious grown
And fearful, as these strange eruptions are.

85 **Casca.** 'Tis Caesar that you mean. Is it not, Cassius?

Cassius. Let it be who it is. For Romans now
Have thews and limbs like to their ancestors.
But woe the while! our fathers' minds are dead,
And we are governed with our mothers' spirits,
90 Our yoke and sufferance show us womanish.

Casca. Indeed, they say the senators tomorrow
Mean to establish Caesar as king,
And he shall wear his crown by sea and land
In every place save here in Italy.

95 **Cassius.** I know where I will wear this dagger then;
Cassius from bondage will deliver Cassius.
Therein, ye gods, you make the weak most strong;
Therein, ye gods, you tyrants do defeat.
Nor stony tower, nor walls of beaten brass,
100 Nor airless dungeon, nor strong links of iron,
Can be retentive to the strength of spirit;
But life, being weary of these worldly bars,
Never lacks power to dismiss itself.
If I know this, know all the world besides,
105 That part of tyranny that I do bear
I can shake off at pleasure.

[Thunder still.]

Casca.   So can I.
So every bondman in his own hand bears
The power to cancel his captivity.

110 **Cassius.** And why should Caesar be a tyrant then?

118-120 **But, O . . . bondman:** Cassius pretends that he did not mean to speak so freely. Maybe, he says, he has been speaking to a happy slave **(willing bondman)** of Caesar.

124 **fleering telltale:** sneering tattletale.

125-127 **Be factious . . . farthest:** Form a group, or faction, to correct **(redress)** these wrongs, and I will go as far as any other man.

133-134 **by this . . . Porch:** Right now, they wait **(stay)** for me at the entrance to the theater Pompey built.

136-138 **the complexion . . . terrible:** The sky **(element)** looks like the work we have ahead of us—bloody, full of fire, and terrible.

140 **gait:** manner of walking.

143-144 **it is . . . stayed for:** This is Casca, who is now part of our plan **(incorporate / To our attempts).** Are they waiting for me?

Poor man! I know he would not be a wolf
But that he sees the Romans are but sheep;
He were no lion, were not Romans hinds.
Those that with haste will make a mighty fire
115 Begin it with weak straws. What trash is Rome,
What rubbish and what offal, when it serves
For the base matter to illuminate
So vile a thing as Caesar! But, O grief,
Where hast thou led me? I, perhaps, speak this
120 Before a willing bondman. Then I know
My answer must be made. But I am armed,
And dangers are to me indifferent.

Casca. You speak to Casca, and to such a man
That is no fleering telltale. Hold, my hand.
125 Be factious for redress of all these griefs,
And I will set this foot of mine as far
As who goes farthest.

Cassius.   There's a bargain made.
Now know you, Casca, I have moved already
130 Some certain of the noblest-minded Romans
To undergo with me an enterprise
Of honorable-dangerous consequence;
And I do know, by this they stay for me
In Pompey's Porch; for now, this fearful night,
135 There is no stir or walking in the streets,
And the complexion of the element
In favor's like the work we have in hand,
Most bloody, fiery, and most terrible.

[Enter Cinna.]

Casca. Stand close awhile, for here come one in haste.

140 **Cassius.** 'Tis Cinna. I do know him by his gait.
He is a friend. Cinna, where haste you so?

Cinna. To find out you. Who's that? Metellus Cimber?

Cassius. No, it is Casca, one incorporate

151-155 Cassius gives Cinna several notes addressed to Brutus, along with instructions about where each note should be placed.

152 *lay it . . . chair:* Place this paper in the judge's *(praetor's)* seat.

159-160 *I will . . . bade me:* I'll hurry *(hie)* to place *(bestow)* these papers as you instructed me.

163-165 *Three parts . . . yields him ours:* We've already won over three parts of Brutus. The next time we meet him, he will be ours completely. *Do you think Brutus will fall for this trick?*

166-169 *he sits . . . worthiness:* The people love Brutus. What would seem offensive if we did it will, like magic *(alchemy),* become good and worthy because of his involvement. *Do you agree with Casca?*

172 *conceited:* judged.

To our attempts. Am I not stayed for, Cinna?

145 **Cinna.** I am glad on't. What a fearful night is this!
There's two or three of us have seen strange sights.

Cassius. Am I not stayed for? Tell me.

Cinna.   Yes, you are.
O Cassius, if you could
150 But win the noble Brutus to our party—

Cassius. Be you content. Good Cinna, take this paper
And look you lay it in the praetor's chair,
Where Brutus may but find it, and throw this
In at his window. Set this up with wax
155 Upon old Brutus' statue. All this done,
Repair to Pompey's Porch, where you shall find us.
Is Decius Brutus and Trebonius there?

Cinna. All but Metellus Cimber, and he's gone
To seek you at your house. Well, I will hie
160 And so bestow these papers as you bade me.

Cassius. That done, repair to Pompey's Theater.

[Exit Cinna.]

Come, Casca, you and I will yet ere day
See Brutus at his house. Three parts of him
Is ours already, and the man entire
165 Upon the next encounter yields him ours.

Casca. O, he sits high in all the people's hearts,
And that which would appear offense in us,
His countenance, like richest alchemy,
Will change to virtue and to worthiness.

170 **Cassius.** Him and his worth and our great need of
him
You have right well conceited. Let us go,
For it is after midnight, and ere day
We will awake him and be sure of him.

[Exeunt.]

2-3 *I cannot . . . day:* There are no stars in the sky to tell me how near it is to morning.

4 *I would . . . soundly:* I wish I could sleep so soundly.

7 *taper:* candle.

10-35 Brutus, alone again, thinks out loud about the problem of Caesar. In general, Brutus fears that Caesar will become too powerful.

10-12 *It must . . . general:* It can only be solved by Caesar's death. I have no personal grudge against him; I'm thinking only of the general welfare.

ACT TWO

Scene 1 *Brutus' orchard in Rome.*

*It is a few hours before dawn on March 15—
the ides of March. Brutus, unable to sleep,
walks in his garden. He faces a crucial
decision: either to continue living under the
tyranny of Caesar or to kill Caesar and thus
end his rule. While considering the problem,
Brutus receives an anonymous letter (from
Cassius) suggesting that Brutus take action
against Caesar. Shortly after, Cassius and the
conspirators visit Brutus, and they all agree to
assassinate Caesar that day.*

Brutus. What, Lucius, ho!
   I cannot by the progress of the stars
   Give guess how near to day. Lucius, I say!
   I would it were my fault to sleep so soundly.
5   When, Lucius, when? Awake, I say! What, Lucius!

[Enter Lucius *from the house.]*

Lucius. Called you, my lord?

Brutus. Get me a taper in my study, Lucius.
   When it is lighted, come and call me here.

Lucius. I will, my lord.

[Exit.]

[Brutus returns to his brooding.]

10 **Brutus.** It must be by his death; and for my part,
   I know no personal cause to spurn at him,
   But for the general. He would be crowned.

15-16 *It is . . . walking:* Sunshine brings out the poisonous snake *(adder),* so walk carefully.

19-28 *The abuse . . . may:* Greatness is misused when it separates pity *(disjoins / Remorse)* from power. I have never known Caesar to be ruled by his heart rather than his head. *What does Brutus think Caesar will do if he gets to the top of* **ambition's ladder?** *What will Caesar's attitude be toward those at the ladder's lower rungs* **(base degrees)?**

29-35 *lest . . . shell:* Rather than let Caesar do that, I should take steps to prevent it. Since our case against Caesar is weak *(Will bear no color)* at present, we must shape *(Fashion)* our argument against him in the following way: We know what kind of person Caesar is now. If his true nature were allowed to develop *(augmented),* it would reach terrible extremes. So we must treat him as a serpent's egg and kill him before he hatches.

36 *closet:* private room.

How that might change his nature, there's the
    question.
15 It is the bright day that brings forth the adder,
    And that craves wary walking. Crown him that,
    And then I grant we put a sting in him
    That at his will he may do danger with.
    The abuse of greatness is when it disjoins
20 Remorse from power. And to speak truth of Caesar,
    I have not known when his affections swayed
    More than his reason. But 'tis a common proof
    That lowliness is young ambition's ladder,
    Whereto the climber-upward turns his face;
25 But when he once attains the upmost round,
    He then unto the ladder turns his back,
    Looks in the clouds, scorning the base degrees
    By which he did ascend. So Caesar may.
    Then lest he may, prevent. And since the quarrel
30 Will bear no color for the thing he is,
    Fashion it thus: that what he is, augmented,
    Would run to these and these extremities;
    And therefore think him as a serpent's egg,
    Which, hatched, would as his kind grow mischievous,
35 And kill him in the shell.

[Reenter Lucius with a letter.]

Lucius. The taper burneth in your closet, sir.
    Searching the window for a flint, I found
    This paper, thus sealed up, and I am sure
    It did not lie there when I went to bed.

[Gives him the letter.]

40 **Brutus.** Get you to bed again; it is not day.
    Is not tomorrow, boy, the ides of March?

Lucius. I know not, sir.

Brutus. Look in the calendar and bring me word.

Lucius. I will, sir.

45 *exhalations:* meteors.

47-48 *etc.:* and so forth; ***redress:*** right a wrong. The letter is meant to suggest certain things to Brutus, without actually spelling them out.

50 *instigations:* suggestions.

52 *Thus . . . out:* I must guess the rest of the sentence.

53 *Shall . . . awe:* Should Rome have such fear and respect for just one man?

55-56 *My ancestors . . . king:* Brutus refers to his ancestor who drove out Rome's last king. After that, rule by the Senate was established.

58-60 *I make . . . Brutus:* I promise you, Rome, if a remedy for our troubles can follow from my action, you will get what you need from Brutus.

63 *whet me:* sharpen my appetite.

65-71 *Between . . . insurrection:* The time between the earliest thought of a terrible act and the actual performance of it is a nightmare. The soul *(genius)* and body *(mortal instruments)* debate the subject, while the man himself feels like a kingdom undergoing a civil war. *What is Brutus' internal conflict?*

[Exit.]

45 **Brutus.** The exhalations, whizzing in the air,
Give so much light that I may read by them.

[Opens the letter and reads.]

"Brutus, thou sleep'st. Awake, and see thyself!
Shall Rome, etc. Speak, strike, redress!"
"Brutus, thou sleep'st. Awake!"
50 Such instigations have been often dropped
Where I have took them up.
"Shall Rome, etc." Thus must I piece it out:
Shall Rome stand under one man's awe? What,
    Rome?
55 My ancestors did from the streets of Rome
The Tarquin drive when he was called a king.
"Speak, strike, redress!" Am I entreated
To speak and strike? O Rome, I make thee promise,
If the redress will follow, thou receivest
60 Thy full petition at the hand of Brutus!

[Reenter Lucius.]

Lucius. Sir, March is wasted fifteen days.

[Knocking within.]

Brutus. 'Tis good. Go to the gate, somebody knocks.

[Exit Lucius.]

Since Cassius first did whet me against Caesar,
I have not slept.
65 Between the acting of a dreadful thing
And the first motion, all the interim is
Like a phantasma or a hideous dream.
The genius and the mortal instruments
Are then in council, and the state of man,
70 Like to a little kingdom, suffers then
The nature of an insurrection.

[Reenter Lucius.]

72 *brother:* Cassius, the husband of Brutus' sister, is his brother-in-law.

79-80 *by no . . . favor:* There is no way I can tell who they are.

82-91 *O conspiracy . . . prevention:* If these plotters are afraid to be seen at night, how will they keep these terrible plans from showing on their faces during the day? They must smile and show friendliness *(affability).* If they go out showing their true natures *(native semblance),* even the dark gateway to hell *(Erebus* er' ə bəs*)* couldn't hide them.

92 *I think . . . rest:* I think we may have come too early.

Lucius. Sir, 'tis your brother Cassius at the door,
Who doth desire to see you.

Brutus.   Is he alone?

75 **Lucius.** No, sir, there are more with him.

Brutus.   Do you know them?

Lucius. No, sir. Their hats are plucked about their ears
And half their faces buried in their cloaks,
That by no means I may discover them
80 By any mark of favor.

Brutus.   Let 'em enter.

[Exit Lucius.]

They are the faction. O conspiracy,
Sham'st thou to show thy dang'rous brow by night,
When evils are most free? O, then by day
85 Where wilt thou find a cavern dark enough
To mask thy monstrous visage? Seek none,
        conspiracy,
Hide it in smiles and affability!
For if thou path, thy native semblance on,
90 No Erebus itself were dim enough
To hide thee from prevention.

[Enter the conspirators, Cassius, Casca, Decius, Cinna,
Metellus Cimber, *and* Trebonius.*]*

Cassius. I think we are too bold upon your rest.
Good morrow, Brutus. Do we trouble you?

Brutus. I have been up this hour, awake all night.
95 Know I these men that come along with you?

Cassius. Yes, every man of them; and no man here
But honors you; and every one doth wish
You had but that opinion of yourself
Which every noble Roman bears of you.
100 This is Trebonius.

107-108 ***What watchful . . . night:*** What troubles keep you
awake at night?

109 ***Shall I entreat a word:*** Cassius asks Brutus to step
aside and talk privately with him. While they talk, the
others chatter about the sky (lines 108-118),
pretending to be not at all interested in what Cassius
and Brutus are discussing.

114 ***fret:*** stripe.

117-118 ***Which is . . . year:*** from a southerly direction, since it
is still early in the year.

124-129 ***If not . . . lottery:*** We do not need to swear our
loyalty to one another. The sadness of people's faces,
our own suffering, and the awful time we live in—if
these aren't strong enough to hold us together, then let
us all go back to bed. In that case, let tyranny live,
while we die off, one at a time, by chance ***(by lottery).***

Brutus. He is welcome hither.

Cassius. This, Decius Brutus.

Brutus. He is welcome too.

Cassius. This, Casca; this, Cinna; and this, Metellus
105 Cimber.

Brutus. They are all welcome.
What watchful cares do interpose themselves
Betwixt your eyes and night?

Cassius. Shall I entreat a word?

[They whisper.]

110 **Decius.** Here lies the east. Doth not the day break
here?

Casca. No.

Cinna. O, pardon, sir, it doth; and yon grey lines
That fret the clouds are messengers of day.

115 **Casca.** You shall confess that you are both deceived.
Here, as I point my sword, the sun arises,
Which is a great way growing on the south,
Weighing the youthful season of the year.
Some two months hence, up higher toward the north
120 He first presents his fire; and the high east
Stands as the Capitol, directly here.

[Brutus and Cassius rejoin the others.]

Brutus. Give me your hands all over, one by one.

Cassius. And let us swear our resolution.

Brutus. No, not on oath. If not the face of men,
125 The sufferance of our souls, the time's abuse—
If these be motives weak, break off betimes,
And every man hence to his idle bed.
So let high-sighted tyranny range on
Till each man drop by lottery. But if these

133-138 *What does Brutus believe is even stronger than any oath the men could take together? Do you agree?*

136 *palter:* go back on our word.

139-150 *Swear . . . from him:* Swearing oaths is for priests, cowards, crafty *(cautelous)* men, old dying men *(feeble carrions)*, and unhappy people who enjoy lying. Such people do not have our unfailing courage *(insuppressive mettle)*. What we believe or what we are about to do *(or our cause or our performance)* does not need oaths, since our blood would not be truly Roman (would be *guilty of a several bastardy*) if any of us were to break his word. Brutus seems to believe that the other conspirators are as honorable as he is. *Do you agree with him?*

151 *sound him:* see what he thinks of the matter.

155-160 *let us . . . gravity:* Let us get Cicero to join us. His age *(silver hairs)* will win us popular support. People will say our youth and wildness were ruled by his sound judgment. So let us tell him of our plan.

130 (As I am sure they do) bear fire enough
To kindle cowards and to steel with valor
The melting spirits of women, then, countrymen,
What need we any spur but our own cause
To prick us to redress? what other bond
135 Than secret Romans that have spoke the word
And will not palter? and what other oath
Than honesty to honesty engaged
That this shall be, or we will fall for it?
Swear priests and cowards and men cautelous,
140 Old feeble carrions and such suffering souls
That welcome wrongs; unto bad causes swear
Such creatures as men doubt; but do not stain
The even virtue of our enterprise,
Nor the insuppressive mettle of our spirits,
145 To think that or our cause or our performance
Did need an oath when every drop of blood
That every Roman bears, and noble bears,
Is guilty of a several bastardy
If he do break the smallest particle
150 Of any promise that hath passed from him.

Cassius. But what of Cicero? Shall we sound him?
I think he will stand very strong with us.

Casca. Let us not leave him out.

Cinna.   No, by no means.

155 **Metellus.** O, let us have him! for his silver hairs
Will purchase us a good opinion
And buy men's voices to commend our deeds.
It shall be said his judgment ruled our hands;
Our youths and wildness shall no whit appear,
160 But all be buried in his gravity.

Brutus. O, name him not! Let us not break with him,
For he will never follow anything
That other men begin.

Cassius.   Then leave him out.

167-173 *I think . . . together:* Shall we also kill Mark Antony, Caesar's good friend? He is a clever plotter *(shrewd contriver)*, and if we had more power *(his means / If he improve them)*, he could be trouble for us.

179 *How does this line reveal a contrast between Brutus' and Cassius' attitudes toward the plot?*

182-183 *O that . . . Caesar:* Brutus wishes they could remove Caesar's soul without having to destroy his body.

187 *Not . . . hounds:* Let's not chop him up like the body of an animal to be fed to dogs.

188-193 *let our hearts . . . murderers:* Let our hearts treat our hands *(servants)* the way sly masters do; we will let our hands do our dirty work, then later scold *(chide)* them for what they have done. This attitude will make us seem to the public *(common eyes)* to be healers *(purgers)* instead of murderers.

198 *ingrafted:* deep-rooted.

165 **Casca.** Indeed he is not fit.

Decius. Shall no man else be touched but only Caesar?

Cassius. Decius, well urged. I think it is not meet
Mark Antony, so well beloved of Caesar,
Should outlive Caesar. We shall find of him
170 A shrewd contriver; and you know, his means,
If he improve them, may well stretch so far
As to annoy us all; which to prevent,
Let Antony and Caesar fall together.

Brutus. Our course will seem too bloody, Caius
175   Cassius,
To cut the head off and then hack the limbs,
Like wrath in death and envy afterwards;
For Antony is but a limb of Caesar.
Let us be sacrificers, but not butchers, Caius.
180 We all stand up against the spirit of Caesar,
And in the spirit of men there is no blood.
O that we then could come by Caesar's spirit
And not dismember Caesar! But, alas,
Caesar must bleed for it! And, gentle friends,
185 Let's kill him boldly, but not wrathfully;
Let's carve him as a dish fit for the gods,
Not hew him as a carcass fit for hounds.
And let our hearts, as subtle masters do,
Stir up their servants to an act of rage
190 And after seem to chide 'em. This shall make
Our purpose necessary, and not envious;
Which so appearing to the common eyes,
We shall be called purgers, not murderers.
And for Mark Antony, think not of him;
195 For he can do no more than Caesar's arm
When Caesar's head is off.

Cassius.   Yet I fear him,
For in the ingrafted love he bears to Caesar—

Brutus. Alas, good Cassius, do not think of him!

202-203 *And that . . . company:* Mark Antony isn't likely to kill himself; he loves sports, wildness, and socializing too much to do such a thing.

204 *There is no fear in him:* We have nothing to fear from Antony. *Do you agree?*

209-217 *But it is . . . Capitol today:* We don't know if Caesar will leave his house *(come forth)* today. Lately he has become superstitious, in contrast to the strong views *(main opinion)* he once had of such beliefs. The cause may be these strange events and the arguments of his fortunetellers *(augurers).* These things may keep him from coming to the Capitol today.

219 *o'ersway him:* change his mind.

220-224 *That unicorns . . . flattered:* Decimus tells of ways to trap shrewd animals. He says that Caesar, who loves to hear such stories, can also be trapped—by flattery.

226 *I can give . . . true bent:* I can get him into the right mood.

229 *By the . . . uttermost:* By eight o'clock. Do we all agree that eight is the latest we will be there?

200 If he love Caesar, all that he can do
Is to himself—take thought, and die for Caesar.
And that were much he should; for he is given
To sports, to wildness, and much company.

Trebonius. There is no fear in him. Let him not die,
205 For he will live and laugh at this hereafter.

[Clock strikes.]

Brutus. Peace! Count the clock.

Cassius.   The clock hath stricken three.

Trebonius. 'Tis time to part.

Cassius.   But it is doubtful yet
210 Whether Caesar will come forth today or no;
For he is superstitious grown of late,
Quite from the main opinion he held once
Of fantasy, of dreams, and ceremonies.
It may be these apparent prodigies,
215 The unaccustomed terror of this night,
And the persuasion of his augurers
May hold him from the Capitol today.

Decius. Never fear that. If he be so resolved,
I can o'ersway him; for he loves to hear
220 That unicorns may be betrayed with trees
And bears with glasses, elephants with holes,
Lions with toils, and men with flatterers;
But when I tell him he hates flatterers,
He says he does, being then most flattered.
225 Let me work,
For I can give his humor the true bent,
And I will bring him to the Capitol.

Cassius. Nay, we will all of us be there to fetch him.

Brutus. By the eighth hour. Is that the uttermost?

230 **Cinna.** Be that the uttermost, and fail not then.

231-233 *Caius . . . of him:* Caius Ligarius has a grudge against Caesar, who criticized him for supporting Pompey. I don't know why you haven't asked him to join our plot.

236 *fashion:* persuade.

243 *Let not . . . purposes:* Let's not let our appearances give away *(put on)* what we are planning to do.

246 All the other conspirators leave, and Brutus is once again alone in his garden.

252 As you read the conversation between Brutus and his wife, think about the kind of relationship they have.

Metellus. Caius Ligarius doth bear Caesar hard,
Who rated him for speaking well of Pompey.
I wonder none of you have thought of him.

Brutus. Now, good Metellus, go along by him.
235 He loves me well, and I have given him reasons.
Send him but hither, and I'll fashion him.

Cassius. The morning comes upon's. We'll leave you,
Brutus.
And, friends, disperse yourselves; but all remember
240 What you have said and show yourselves true
Romans.

Brutus. Good gentlemen, look fresh and merrily.
Let not our looks put on our purposes,
But bear it as our Roman actors do,
245 With untired spirits and formal constancy.
And so good morrow to you every one.

[Exeunt all but Brutus.]

Boy! Lucius! Fast asleep? It is no matter.
Enjoy the honey-heavy dew of slumber.
Thou hast no figures nor no fantasies
250 Which busy care draws in the brains of men;
Therefore thou sleep'st so sound.

[Enter Portia, Brutus' wife.]

Portia.   Brutus, my lord!

Brutus. Portia! What mean you? Wherefore rise you
now?
255 It is not for your health thus to commit
Your weak condition to the raw cold morning.

Portia. Nor for yours neither. Y'have ungently, Brutus,
Stole from my bed. And yesternight at supper
You suddenly arose and walked about,
260 Musing and sighing with your arms across;
And when I asked you what the matter was,

265 **Yet:** still.

266 **wafture:** gesture.

269 **withal:** also.

270 **humor:** mood.

273-275 **And could . . . you Brutus:** If a mood like that could change your appearance **(shape)** the way it changes your personality **(condition),** I would not recognize you.

277 *Why do you think Brutus lies to Portia?*

281-287 **Is Brutus . . . sickness:** Do you expect me to believe that you're sick? Is it healthy to walk without a coat **(unbraced)** and breathe the air of a damp morning or the unhealthy night air that is not yet cleansed **(unpurged)** by the sun?

288-290 **You have . . . know of:** You have a sickness of the mind; as your wife, I have a right to know what it is.

295 **heavy:** sad.

You stared upon me with ungentle looks.
I urged you further, then you scratched your head
And too impatiently stamped with your foot.
265 Yet I insisted, yet you answered not,
But with an angry wafture of your hand
Gave sign for me to leave you. So I did,
Fearing to strengthen that impatience
Which seemed too much enkindled, and withal
270 Hoping it was but an effect of humor,
Which sometime hath his hour with every man.
It will not let you eat nor talk nor sleep,
And could it work so much upon your shape
As it hath much prevailed on your condition,
275 I should not know you Brutus. Dear my lord,
Make me acquainted with your cause of grief.

Brutus. I am not well in health, and that is all.

Portia. Brutus is wise and, were he not in health,
He would embrace the means to come by it.

280 **Brutus.** Why, so I do. Good Portia, go to bed.

Portia. Is Brutus sick, and is it physical
To walk unbraced and suck up the humors
Of the dank morning? What, is Brutus sick,
And will he steal out of his wholesome bed
285 To dare the vile contagion of the night,
And tempt the rheumy and unpurgéd air,
To add unto his sickness? No, my Brutus.
You have some sick offense within your mind,
Which by the right and virtue of my place
290 I ought to know of; and upon my knees
I charm you, by my once commended beauty,
By all your vows of love, and that great vow
Which did incorporate and make us one,
That you unfold to me, yourself, your half,
295 Why you are heavy, and what men tonight
Have had resort to you; for here have been
Some six or seven, who did hide their faces

303 *appertain:* relate.

304 *in sort or limitation:* only in part.

311-312 *the ruddy . . . heart:* my blood.

319-325 *Think you . . . secrets:* How can you consider me merely a typical woman, when I am the daughter of Cato (a highly respected Roman) and the wife of Brutus? So tell me your secret. I have proven my strength by wounding myself here in the thigh. If I can put up with that pain, I can certainly deal with my husband's secrets. *Should Brutus tell Portia his secret?*

Even from darkness.

Brutus.   Kneel not, gentle Portia.

300 **Portia.** I should not need if you were gentle Brutus.
   Within the bond of marriage, tell me, Brutus,
   Is it excepted I should know no secrets
   That appertain to you? Am I yourself
   But, as it were, in sort or limitation?
305 To keep with you at meals, comfort your bed,
   And talk to you sometimes? Dwell I but in the
      suburbs
   Of your good pleasure? If it be no more,
   Portia is Brutus' harlot, not his wife.

310 **Brutus.** You are my true and honorable wife,
   As dear to me as are the ruddy drops
   That visit my sad heart.

   Portia. If this were true, then should I know this
      secret.
315 I grant I am a woman, but withal
   A woman that Lord Brutus took to wife.
   I grant that I am a woman, but withal
   A woman well reputed, Cato's daughter.
   Think you I am no stronger than my sex,
320 Being so fathered and so husbanded?
   Tell me your counsels; I will not disclose 'em.
   I have made strong proof of my constancy,
   Giving myself a voluntary wound
   Here, in the thigh. Can I bear that with patience,
325 And not my husband's secrets?

Brutus.   O ye gods,
   Render me worthy of this noble wife!

[Knocking within.]

   Hark, hark! one knocks. Portia, go in awhile,
   And by-and-by thy bosom shall partake
330 The secrets of my heart.

331-332 *All my . . . brows:* I will explain all my dealings and the reason for my sad looks.

338 *Vouchsafe . . . tongue:* Accept a good morning from a sick man.

341 *kerchief:* a covering to protect the head during sickness.

343 *exploit:* deed.

347 *I here discard my sickness:* I declare myself cured.

348 *derived . . . loins:* descended from noble Romans.

349 *exorcist:* someone who can call up spirits.

355 *What does Caius mean?*

All my engagements I will construe to thee,
All the charactery of my sad brows.
Leave me with haste.

[Exit Portia.]

Lucius, who's that knocks?

[Reenter Lucius with Caius-Ligarius.]

335 **Lucius.** Here is a sick man that would speak with you.

Brutus. Caius Ligarius, that Metellus spake of.
Boy, stand aside. Caius Ligarius, how?

Caius. Vouchsafe good morrow from a feeble tongue.

Brutus. O, what a time have you chose out, brave
340   Caius,
To wear a kerchief! Would you were not sick!

Caius. I am not sick if Brutus have in hand
Any exploit worthy the name of honor.

Brutus. Such an exploit have I in hand, Ligarius,
345   Had you a healthful ear to hear of it.

Caius. By all the gods that Romans bow before,
I here discard my sickness! Soul of Rome!
Brave son, derived from honorable loins!
Thou like an exorcist has conjured up
350   My mortified spirit. Now bid me run,
And I will strive with things impossible;
Yea, get the better of them. What's to do?

Brutus. A piece of work that will make sick men
whole.

355 **Caius.** But are not some whole that we must make
sick?

Brutus. That must we also. What it is, my Caius,
I shall unfold to thee as we are going
To whom it must be done.

360 *Set on your foot:* Lead the way.

362 *it sufficeth:* It is enough.

6-7 *Go bid . . . success:* Roman priests would kill an animal as a sacrifice to the gods. Then they would cut the animal open and examine its internal organs for signs of future events.

360 **Caius.**   Set on your foot,
And with a heart new-fired I follow you,
To do I know not what; but it sufficeth
That Brutus leads me on.

[Thunder.]

Brutus.   Follow me then.

[Exeunt.]

Scene 2 *Caesar's house in Rome.*

It is now past dawn on March 15. Like everyone else in Rome, Caesar and his wife have slept badly because of the storm. There is still some lightning and thunder. Caesar prepares to go to the Capitol, but because of the many threatening omens, his wife Calpurnia insists that he stay home. Caesar agrees, for Calpurnia's sake. He changes his mind when Decius, one of the conspirators, persuades him that he must not seem swayed by his wife's superstitions. Although Caesar doesn't know it, the other conspirators are on their way to his house to make sure he does not decide to stay at home.

[Enter Caesar in his nightgown.]

Caesar. Nor heaven nor earth have been at peace
    tonight.
Thrice hath Calpurnia in her sleep cried out
"Help, ho! They murder Caesar!" Who's within?

[Enter a Servant.]

5 **Servant.** My lord?

Caesar. Go bid the priests do present sacrifice,
And bring me their opinions of success.

Servant. I will, my lord.

[Exit.]

12-62 As you read this conversation, think about Caesar's view of himself. Remember the way he talked of himself to Antony in Act One. Look for new evidence of Caesar's view of his own importance and his power.

12-14 *The things . . . vanished:* When I turn to face the things that threaten me, they disappear.

15-28 *Caesar, I never . . . fear them:* Calpurnia tells Caesar that she has never before believed in omens *(stood on ceremonies),* but now she is frightened. She describes the terrible things she has heard of from the men who were on guard during the night.

27 *beyond all use:* unlike anything we are accustomed to.

29-32 Caesar insists that, if these are omens and if the gods have destined that certain things will happen, no one can avoid them. He will go out, since the predictions, he believes, apply to the whole world, not only to Caesar.

[Enter Caesar's wife Calpurnia, alarmed.]

Calpurnia. What mean you, Caesar? Think you to
10   walk forth?
You shall not stir out of your house today.

Caesar. Caesar shall forth. The things that threatened me
Ne'er looked but on my back. When they shall see
The face of Caesar, they are vanished.

15 **Calpurnia.** Caesar, I never stood on ceremonies,
Yet now they fright me. There is one within,
Besides the things that we have heard and seen,
Recounts most horrid sights seen by the watch.
A lioness hath whelped in the streets,
20 And graves have yawned and yielded up their dead.
Fierce fiery warriors fought upon the clouds
In ranks and squadrons and right form of war,
Which drizzled blood upon the Capitol.
The noise of battle hurtled in the air,
25 Horses did neigh, and dying men did groan,
And ghosts did shriek and squeal about the streets.
O Caesar, these things are beyond all use,
And I do fear them!

Caesar.   What can be avoided
30 Whose end is purposed by the mighty gods?
Yet Caesar shall go forth, for these predictions
Are to the world in general as to Caesar.

Calpurnia. When beggars die there are no comets seen;
The heavens themselves blaze forth the death of
35   princes.

Caesar. Cowards die many times before their deaths;
The valiant never taste of death but once.
Of all the wonders that I yet have heard,
It seems to me most strange that men should fear,
40 Seeing that death, a necessary end,
Will come when it will come.

[Reenter Servant.]

51 *littered in one day:* born at the same time.

72-75 *Shall . . . not come:* Caesar is appalled by his wife's
suggestion that he lie to a bunch of old men
(greybeards) about his reason for not going to the
Senate. *How might an actor say these lines?*

What say the augurers?

Servant. They would not have you to stir forth today.
Plucking the entrails of an offering forth,
45   They could not find a heart within the beast.

Caesar. The gods do this in shame of cowardice.
Caesar should be a beast without a heart
If he should stay at home today for fear.
No, Caesar shall not. Danger knows full well
50   That Caesar is more dangerous than he.
We are two lions littered in one day,
And I the elder and more terrible,
And Caesar shall go forth.

Calpurnia.   Alas, my lord!
55   Your wisdom is consumed in confidence.
Do not go forth today. Call it my fear
That keeps you in the house and not your own.
We'll send Mark Antony to the Senate House,
And he shall say you are not well today.
60   Let me upon my knee prevail in this.

Caesar. Mark Antony shall say I am not well,
And for thy humor I will stay at home.

[Enter Decius.]

Here's Decius Brutus, he shall tell them so.

Decius. Caesar, all hail! Good morrow, worthy Caesar!
65   I come to fetch you to the Senate House.

Caesar. And you are come in very happy time
To bear my greetings to the senators
And tell them that I will not come today.
Cannot, is false; and that I dare not, falser.
70   I will not come today. Tell them so, Decius.

Calpurnia. Say he is sick.

Caesar.   Shall Caesar send a lie?
Have I in conquest stretched mine arm so far

87 *portents:* signs of evil to come.

90-97 Decius has to think fast. He promised the others that he could flatter Caesar into believing anything. Now he must give Caesar a new interpretation of Calpurnia's dream, one that will get him out of the house.

90 *amiss:* wrongly.

95-96 *great men . . . cognizance:* Great men will come to you for honors and souvenirs to remember you by.

103-104 *it were . . . rendered:* It's likely that someone will make a sarcastic comment.

To be afeard to tell greybeards the truth?
75 Decius, go tell them Caesar will not come.

Decius. Most mighty Caesar, let me know some cause,
Lest I be laughed at when I tell them so.

Caesar. The cause is in my will: I will not come.
That is enough to satisfy the Senate;
80 But for your private satisfaction,
Because I love you, I will let you know.
Calpurnia here, my wife, stays me at home.
She dreamt tonight she saw my statue,
Which, like a fountain with an hundred spouts,
85 Did run pure blood, and many lusty Romans
Came smiling and did bathe their hands in it.
And these does she apply for warnings and portents
And evils imminent, and on her knee
Hath begged that I will stay at home today.

90 **Decius.** This dream is all amiss interpreted;
It was a vision fair and fortunate.
Your statue spouting blood in many pipes,
In which so many smiling Romans bathed,
Signifies that from you great Rome shall suck
95 Reviving blood, and that great men shall press
For tinctures, stains, relics, and cognizance.
This by Calpurnia's dream is signified.

Caesar. And this way have you well expounded it.

Decius. I have, when you have heard what I can say:
100 And know it now, the Senate have concluded
To give this day a crown to mighty Caesar.
If you shall send them word you will not come,
Their minds may change. Besides, it were a mock
Apt to be rendered, for some one to say
105 "Break up the Senate till another time,
When Caesar's wife shall meet with better dreams."
If Caesar hide himself, shall they not whisper
"Lo, Caesar is afraid"?

109-111 ***my dear . . . liable:*** My sincere interest in your career
(proceeding) makes me tell you this. My feeling for
you overtakes my intelligence ***(reason).*** *What
arguments does Decius use to change Caesar's mind?*

122 ***ague:*** sickness.

126-127 ***Antony . . . up:*** Even Antony, who parties ***(revels)***
late into the night, is up early today.

135 ***Aside:*** privately, in a way that keeps the other
characters from hearing what is said. Think of it as a
whisper that the audience happens to overhear.

Pardon me, Caesar, for my dear dear love
110 To your proceeding bids me tell you this,
And reason to my love is liable.

Caesar. How foolish do your fears seem now,
Calpurnia!
I am ashamed I did yield to them.
115 Give me my robe, for I will go.

[Enter Brutus, Ligarius, Metellus, Casca, Trebonius, Cinna, and Publius.]

And look where Publius is come to fetch me.

Publius. Good morrow, Caesar.

Caesar.   Welcome Publius.
What Brutus, are you stirred so early too?
120 Good morrow, Casca. Caius Ligarius,
Caesar was ne'er so much your enemy
As that same ague which hath made you lean.
What is't o'clock?

Brutus.   Caesar, 'tis strucken eight.

125 **Caesar.** I thank you for your pains and courtesy.

[Enter Antony.]

See! Antony, that revels long o'nights,
Is notwithstanding up. Good morrow, Antony.

Antony. So to most noble Caesar.

Caesar.   Bid them prepare within.
130 I am to blame to be thus waited for.
Now, Cinna, now, Metellus. What, Trebonius!
I have an hour's talk in store for you;
Remember that you call on me today;
Be near me, that I may remember you.

135 **Trebonius.** Caesar, I will. *[Aside]* And so near will I be
That your best friends shall wish I had been further.

140-142 ***The every . . . upon:*** The fact that we behave like friends doesn't mean we are friends. My heart grieves ***(yearns)*** to think of it. *What is Brutus saying about his friendship with Caesar?*

9 ***lover:*** devoted friend.

13-14 ***My heart . . . emulation:*** My heart is sad that Caesar's greatness cannot escape jealousy ***(the teeth of emulation).***

16 ***contrive:*** plot.

Caesar. Good friends, go in and taste some wine with
me,
And we (like friends) will straightway go together.

140 **Brutus.** *[Aside]* That every like is not the same, O
Caesar,
The heart of Brutus yearns to think upon.

[Exeunt.]

Scene 3 *A street in Rome near the Capitol.*

*In this brief scene, Caesar has still another
chance to avoid the path that leads to his death.
Artemidorus, a supporter of Caesar, has learned
about the plot. He reads a letter he has written
to warn Caesar. Then he waits in the street for
Caesar to pass by on his way to the Capitol.*

[Enter Artemidorus, *reading a paper.]*

Artemidorus. "Caesar, beware of Brutus; take heed of
Cassius; come not near Casca; have an eye to Cinna;
trust not Trebonius; mark well Metellus Cimber; Decius Brutus loves thee not; thou hast wronged Caius
5 Ligarius. There is but one mind in all these men,
and it is bent against Caesar. If thou beest not immortal, look about you. Security gives way to
conspiracy. The mighty gods defend thee!
"Thy Lover,
10 "ARTEMIDORUS."
Here will I stand till Caesar pass along
And as a suitor will I give him this.
My heart laments that virtue cannot live
Out of the teeth of emulation.
15 If thou read this, O Caesar, thou mayst live;
If not, the Fates with traitors do contrive.

[Exit.]

5-6 *I would have . . . do there:* I would have had you travel there and back without telling you what I wanted you to do. (Portia is upset with herself for acting foolishly.)

10 *keep counsel:* keep a secret. *What do you think of Portia's (or Shakespeare's) statement that it is hard for a woman to keep a secret?*

17 *what suitors press to him:* what people stand near him.

21 *I heard . . . fray:* Portia imagines that she has heard a noise like a battle *(fray).*

23 *Sooth:* truthfully.

Scene 4 *In front of Brutus' house.*

Shakespeare continues to build suspense with another short scene. This one involves Brutus' wife, Portia, who feels anxious about the conspiracy. Portia nervously orders the servant Lucius to go and see what is happening at the Capitol. She next meets the soothsayer, who makes her even more anxious as he continues to predict danger for Caesar.

[Enter Portia and Lucius.]

Portia. I prithee, boy, run to the Senate House.
Stay not to answer me, but get thee gone!
Why dost thou stay?

Lucius.   To know my errand, madam.

5 **Portia.** I would have had thee there and here again
Ere I can tell thee what thou shouldst do there.
O constancy, be strong upon my side,
Set a huge mountain 'tween my heart and tongue!
I have a man's mind, but a woman's might.
10 How hard it is for women to keep counsel!
Art thou here yet?

Lucius.   Madam, what should I do?
Run to the Capitol and nothing else?
And so return to you and nothing else?

15 **Portia.** Yes, bring me word, boy, if thy lord look well,
For he went sickly forth; and take good note
What Caesar doth, what suitors press to him.
Hark, boy! What noise is that?

Lucius. I hear none, madam.

20 **Portia.**   Prithee, listen well.
I heard a bustling rumor like a fray,
And the wind brings it from the Capitol.

Lucius. Sooth, madam, I hear nothing.

[Enter the Soothsayer.]

24 The soothsayer is the same fortuneteller who warned Caesar to beware the ides of March. He is now on his way to the street near the Capitol building where he usually sits.

32 *Thou hast . . . Caesar:* Have you some favor to ask of Caesar?

38-39 *None . . . chance:* I'm not sure of any danger, but I fear that some may chance to happen.

49-50 *Brutus hath . . . not grant:* Brutus has a favor to ask that Caesar will not give him.

51 *commend . . . lord:* Give my husband my good wishes.

severally: in different directions.

Portia. Come hither, fellow. Which way hast thou
25   been?

Soothsayer. At mine own house, good lady.

Portia. What is't o'clock?

Soothsayer.   About the ninth hour, lady.

Portia. Is Caesar yet gone to the Capitol?

30   **Soothsayer.** Madam, not yet. I go to take my stand,
      To see him pass on to the Capitol.

Portia. Thou hast some suit to Caesar, hast thou not?

Soothsayer. That I have, lady. If it will please Caesar
      To be so good to Caesar as to hear me,
35   I shall beseech him to befriend himself.

Portia. Why, know'st thou any harm's intended
      towards him?

Soothsayer. None that I know will be, much that I
      fear may chance.
40   Good morrow to you. Here the street is narrow.
      The throng that follows Caesar at the heels,
      Of senators, of praetors, common suitors,
      Will crowd a feeble man almost to death.
      I'll get me to a place more void and there
45   Speak to great Caesar as he comes along.

[Exit.]

Portia. I must go in. Ay me, how weak a thing
      The heart of woman is! O Brutus,
      The heavens speed thee in thine enterprise—
      Sure the boy heard me.—Brutus hath a suit
50   That Caesar will not grant.—O, I grow faint.—
      Run, Lucius, and commend me to my Lord;
      Say I am merry. Come to me again
      And bring me word what he doth say to thee.

[Exeunt severally.]

3 *schedule:* document.

4-13 Artemidorus is the man who has prepared a written warning for Caesar to read *(o'erread)* about the men plotting against him. The conspirators suspect this and do not want him to get to Caesar. Decius steps in front of Artemidorus and offers a written request from someone else. Then Publius (who is not a conspirator) and Cassius push Artemidorus aside.

ACT THREE

Scene 1 *The Capitol in Rome.*

Outside the Capitol, Caesar refuses to look at Artemidorus' letter of warning. Caesar next moves into the Capitol. There, the conspirators surround him, pretending to plead a case. Suddenly, they stab him to death. Mark Antony flees, but Brutus persuades the conspirators to let him live. Brutus himself promises to explain the killing and its reasons to the Roman people. Antony returns and pretends to be an ally of the conspirators. Secretly, however, he plans to strike back with help from Octavius Caesar, who is now on his way to Rome.

[The Senate sits on a higher level, waiting for Caesar *to appear.* Artemidorus *and the* Soothsayer *are among the crowd. A flourish of trumpets. Enter* Caesar, Brutus, Cassius, Casca, Decius, Metellus, Trebonius, Cinna, Antony, Lepidus, Popilius, *and others.* Caesar *stops in front of the* Soothsayer.]*

Caesar. The ides of March are come.

Soothsayer. Ay, Caesar, but not gone.

[Artemidorus steps up to Caesar with his warning.]

Artemidorus. Hail, Caesar! Read this schedule.

[Decius steps up quickly with another paper.]

Decius. Trebonius doth desire you to o'erread

5   (At your best leisure) this his humble suit.

Artemidorus. O Caesar, read mine first, for mine's a suit

11 *Sirrah:* a form of address used toward a servant or inferior, often to express anger or disrespect; *give place:* get out of the way.

14 *I wish . . . thrive:* I hope your venture is successful.

20-27 *Look how . . . change:* Brutus and Cassius watch Popilius Lena talk privately with Caesar. They fear he is telling Caesar of their plot. Then, seeing Popilius Lena smile, they know they were mistaken.

That touches Caesar nearer. Read it, great Caesar!

Caesar. What touches us ourself shall be last served.

[Caesar *pushes the paper aside and turns away.*]

Artemidorus. Delay not, Caesar! Read it instantly!

10 **Caesar.** What, is the fellow mad?

Publius.   Sirrah, give place.

[Publius *and other conspirators force* Artemidorus *away from* Caesar.]

Cassius. What, urge you your petitions in the street?
    Come to the Capitol.

[Caesar *goes into the Senate House, the rest following.*
Popilius *speaks to* Cassius *in a low voice.*]

Popilius. I wish your enterprise today may thrive.

15 **Cassius.** What enterprise, Popilius?

Popilius.   Fare you well.

[*Advances to* Caesar.]

Brutus. What said Popilius Lena?

Cassius. He wished today our enterprise might thrive.
    I fear our purpose is discovered.

20 **Brutus.** Look how he makes to Caesar. Mark him.

Cassius. Casca, be sudden, for we fear prevention.
    Brutus, what shall be done? If this be known,
    Cassius or Caesar never shall turn back,
    For I will slay myself.

25 **Brutus.**   Cassius, be constant.
    Popilius Lena speaks not of our purposes,
    For look, he smiles, and Caesar doth not change.

Cassius. Trebonius knows his time, for look you, Brutus,
    He draws Mark Antony out of the way.

31 prefer . . . Caesar: ask his favor of Caesar.

32 Press . . . him: Get near him (Metullus Cimber) and back up his request.

36 puissant: powerful.

40-53 I must prevent . . . satisfied: Caesar claims that, unlike ordinary men, he cannot be moved by bowing and scraping. He will not let such things change the laws of the country **(preordinance and first decree).** His heart cannot be melted by sweet words, bowing **(curtsies),** and behavior fit for a dog **(base spaniel fawning).** Metellus Cimber's brother, Caesar says, has been banished by law. Begging won't change that. *Does Caesar evaluate his own personality correctly?*

59 freedom of repeal: the right to return to Rome from exile.

[Exeunt Antony and Trebonius.]

30 **Decius.** Where is Metellus Cimber? Let him go
And presently prefer his suit to Caesar.

Brutus. He is addressed. Press near and second him.

Cinna. Casca, you are the first that rears your hand.

[Caesar seats himself in his high Senate chair.]

Caesar. Are we all ready? What is now amiss
35 That Caesar and his Senate must redress?

Metellus. Most high, most mighty, and most puissant
    Caesar,
Metellus Cimber throws before thy seat
An humble heart.

[Kneeling.]

40 **Caesar.**   I must prevent three, Cimber.
These couchings and these lowly courtesies
Might fire the blood of ordinary men
And turn preordinance and first decree
Into the law of children. Be not fond
45 To think that Caesar bears such rebel blood
That will be thawed from the true quality
With that which melteth fools—I mean, sweet words,
Low-crookèd curtsies, and base spaniel fawning.
Thy brother by decree is banished.
50 If thou dost bend and pray and fawn for him,
I spurn thee like a cur out of my way.
Know, Caesar doth not wrong, nor without cause
Will he be satisfied.

Metellus. Is there no voice more worthy than my own,
55 To sound more sweetly in great Caesar's ear
For the repealing of my banished brother?

Brutus. I kiss thy hand, but not in flattery, Caesar,
Desiring thee that Publius Cimber may
Have an immediate freedom of repeal.

60-63 Caesar is surprised that Brutus would beg for freedom **(enfranchisement)** for Publius Cimber. Actually, Brutus, like the rest of the conspirators, is only looking for an excuse to carry out their plan.

64-81 *I could be . . . Olympus:* Caesar says he is too strong to be moved by begging, even when it comes from these respected men. He compares himself to the North Star, which sailors use for direction because it always appears at the same place in the sky. Like that star, Caesar says, which has no equal in the sky **(fellow in the firmament),** he cannot be moved. They might as well try to lift Mount Olympus (the mountain where the Greek gods were believed to live). *Is Caesar bragging?*

83 *Doth not . . . kneel:* Can't you see that even Brutus' kneeling doesn't sway me? **Bootless** means "without any effect," like a kick from a foot that has no boot.

85 *Et tu, Brute?:* Even you, Brutus?

88 *Some . . . pulpits:* Some of you go to the speakers' platforms. The scene is now chaos—people yelling, screaming, and running in fear. Cassius and Brutus are trying to avoid a riot.

60 **Caesar.** What, Brutus?

Cassius.   Pardon, Caesar! Caesar, pardon!
　　As low as to thy foot doth Cassius fall
　　To beg enfranchisement for Publius Cimber.

Caesar. I could be well moved, if I were as you;
65 　　If I could pray to move, prayers would move me;
　　But I am constant as the Northern Star,
　　Of whose truth-fixed and resting quality
　　There is no fellow in the firmament.
　　The skies are painted with unnumbered sparks,
70 　　They are all fire, and every one doth shine;
　　But there's but one in all doth hold his place.
　　So in the world: 'tis furnished well with men.
　　And men are flesh and blood, and apprehensive,
　　Yet in the number I do not know but one
75 　　That unassailable holds on his rank,
　　Unshaked of motion; and that I am he,
　　Let me a little show it, even in this,
　　That I was constant Cimber should be banished
　　And constant do remain to keep him so.

80 **Cinna.** O Caesar!

Caesar. Hence! Wilt thou lift up Olympus?

Decius. Great Caesar!

Caesar. Doth not Brutus bootless kneel?

Casca. Speak hands for me!

[They stab Caesar. Casca, *the others in turn, then* Brutus.*]*

85 **Caesar.** *Et tu, Brute?*—Then fall Caesar!

[Dies.]

Cinna. Liberty! Freedom! Tyranny is dead!
　　Run hence, proclaim, cry it about the streets!

Cassius. Some to the common pulpits and cry out
　　"Liberty, freedom, and enfranchisement!"

101-102 *leave . . . mischief:* Cassius wants Publius, an old man, to leave before he gets hurt by the crowd.

103 *abide:* suffer for.

116-121 Brutus leads the others in covering themselves with Caesar's blood. He wants the Romans to think of their act as a public one, an act they are not trying to hide.

90 **Brutus.** People and Senators, be not affrighted.
Fly not; stand still. Ambition's debt is paid.

Casca. Go to the pulpit, Brutus.

Decius. And Cassius, too.

Brutus. Where's Publius?

95 **Cinna.** Here, quite confounded with this mutiny.

Metellus. Stand fast together, lest some friend of Caesar's
Should chance—

Brutus. Talk not of standing! Publius, good cheer.
There is no harm intended to your person
100 Nor to no Roman else. So tell them, Publius.

Cassius. And leave us, Publius, lest that the people,
Rushing on us, should do your age some mischief.

Brutus. Do so, and let no man abide this deed
But we the doers.

[Reenter Trebonius.]

105 **Cassius.** Where is Antony?

Trebonius. Fled to his house amazed.
Men, wives, and children stare, cry out, and run,
As it were doomsday.

Brutus. Fates, we will know your pleasures.
110 That we shall die, we know; 'tis but the time,
And drawing days out, that men stand upon.

Cassius. Why, he that cuts off twenty years of life
Cuts off so many years of fearing death.

Brutus. Grant that, and then is death a benefit.
115 So are we Caesar's friends, that have abridged
His time of fearing death. Stoop, Romans, stoop,
And let us bathe our hands in Caesar's blood
Up to the elbows and besmear our swords.
Then walk we forth, even to the market place,

125 *How many . . . sport:* This scene will often be performed as a play in the future in countries and languages that don't even exist now. *Why do you think Shakespeare added this line?*

126 *Pompey's basis:* the foot of Pompey's statue.

136-149 Fearful for his own life, Antony sends a message with his servant. Lying face down on the floor *(being prostrate),* the servant begs for assurance that Brutus will promise *(vouchsafe)* Antony's safety so that he may come and be given an explanation *(be resolved)* for Caesar's murder. Then Antony will agree to follow Brutus through the dangers of this new, untried government *(the hazards of this untrod state).*

120 And waving our red weapons o'er our heads,
Let's all cry, "Peace, freedom, and liberty!"

Cassius. Stoop then and wash. How many ages hence
Shall this our lofty scene be acted over
In states unborn and accents yet unknown!

125 **Brutus.** How many times shall Caesar bleed in sport,
That now on Pompey's basis lies along
No worthier than the dust!

Cassius. So oft as that shall be.
So often shall the knot of us be called
130 The men that gave their country liberty.

Decius. What, shall we forth?

Cassius. Ay, every man away.
Brutus shall lead, and we will grace his heels
With the most boldest and best hearts of Rome.

[Enter a Servant.]

135 **Brutus.** Soft! who comes here? A friend of Antony's.

Servant. Thus, Brutus, did my master bid me kneel;
Thus did Mark Antony bid me fall down;
And being prostrate, thus he bade me say:
Brutus is noble, wise, valiant, and honest;
140 Caesar was mighty, bold, royal, and loving.
Say I love Brutus and I honor him;
Say I feared Caesar, honored him, and loved him.
If Brutus will vouchsafe that Antony
May safely come to him and be resolved
145 How Caesar hath deserved to lie in death,
Mark Antony shall not love Caesar dead
So well as Brutus living, but will follow
The fortunes and affairs of noble Brutus
Thorough the hazards of this untrod state
150 With all true faith. So says my master Antony.

Brutus. Thy master is a wise and valiant Roman.

153-155 *What promise does Brutus tell the servant to relay to Antony?*

156 ***presently:*** immediately.

158-160 ***But yet . . . purpose:*** Unlike Brutus, Cassius doesn't trust Antony. He adds that his doubts ***(misgiving)*** in matters like this are usually accurate. *Who do you think is right, Cassius or Brutus?*

163-178 The sight of Caesar's body causes Antony to break down. Keep in mind that he truly loved Caesar, almost as a son loves his father.

167-178 ***Who else . . . this age:*** Who else is so diseased ***(rank)*** that he must be "cured" by the knives of the men who just killed Caesar? Antony says he would be honored to be killed at the same time, with the same weapons, and by the same blood- stained ***(purpled)*** hands that killed Caesar. He adds that the honor would come partly from being killed by such great men ***(the choice and master spirits of this age)***. *Do you believe that Antony is being honest here?*

I never thought him worse.
Tell him, so please him come unto this place,
He shall be satisfied and, by my honor,
155 Depart untouched.

Servant.   I'll fetch him presently.

[Exit]

Brutus. I know that we shall have him well to friend.

Cassius. I wish we may. But yet have I a mind
That fears him much; and my misgiving still
160 Falls shrewdly to the purpose.

[Reenter Antony.]

Brutus. But here comes Antony. Welcome, Mark
Antony.

Antony. O mighty Caesar! Dost thou lie so low?
Are all thy conquests, glories, triumphs, spoils,
165 Shrunk to this little measure? Fare thee well.
I know not, gentlemen, what you intend,
Who else must be let blood, who else is rank.
If I myself, there is not hour so fit
As Caesar's death's hour; nor no instrument
170 Of half that worth as those your swords, made rich
With the most noble blood of all this world.
I do beseech ye, if you bear me hard,
Now, whilst your purpled hands do reek and smoke,
Fulfill your pleasure. Live a thousand years,
175 I shall not find myself so apt to die;
No place will please me so, no mean of death,
As here by Caesar, and by you cut off,
The choice and master spirits of this age.

Brutus. O Antony, beg not your death of us!
180 Though now we must appear bloody and cruel,
As by our hands and this our present act
You see we do, yet see you but our hands
And this the bleeding business they have done.

186 *As fire . . . pity:* As one fire consumes another, our sorrow for Rome became greater than our sorrow for Caesar.

188-193 *To you . . . dignities:* As far as you're concerned, Antony, our swords are harmless *(have leaden points).* Our arms, even though they seem cruel *(in strength of malice),* and our hearts, full of brotherly feeling, welcome you. You will have as much to say as anyone in handing out honors from the new government.

208 *credit:* reputation.

209 *conceit:* think of.

212-227 These lines are addressed to the corpse *(corse)* of Caesar. Antony is so upset that he temporarily forgets who is with him.

Our hearts you see not. They are pitiful;
185 And pity to the general wrong of Rome
(As fire drives out fire, so pity pity)
Hath done this deed on Caesar. For your part,
To you our swords have leaden points, Mark Antony.
Our arms in strength of malice, and our hearts
190 Of brothers' temper, do receive you in
With all kind of love, good thoughts, and reverence.

Cassius. Your voice shall be as strong as any man's
In the disposing of new dignities.

Brutus. Only be patient till we have appeased
195 The multitude, beside themselves with fear,
And then we will deliver you the cause
Why I, that did love Caesar when I struck him,
Have thus proceeded.

Antony.   I doubt not of your wisdom.
200 Let each man render me his bloody hand.
First, Marcus Brutus, will I shake with you;
Next, Caius Cassius, do I take your hand;
Now, Decius Brutus, yours; now yours, Metellus;
Yours, Cinna; and, my valiant Casca, yours.
205 Though last, not least in love, yours, good
        Trebonius.
Gentlemen all—Alas, what shall I say?
My credit now stands on such slippery ground
That one of two bad ways you must conceit me,
210 Either a coward or a flatterer.
That I did love thee, Caesar, O, 'tis true!
If then thy spirit look upon us now,
Shall it not grieve thee dearer than thy death
To see thy Antony making his peace,
215 Shaking the bloody fingers of thy foes,
Most noble! in the presence of thy corse?
Had I as many eyes as thou hast wounds,
Weeping as fast as they stream forth thy blood,
It would become me better than to close

221 *Here . . . hart:* This is the place where you were trapped *(bayed)* like a hunted deer *(hart).*

223 *Signed . . . lethe:* Marked with your blood *(spoil)* and red in your death. At this point, Antony is probably having difficulty speaking through his tears.

229-231 With these lines, Antony regains control of himself. He points out that even Caesar's enemies will say such things as he has just said.

233 *compact:* agreement.

234 *pricked:* listed; marked by punching a hole in a wax tablet.

236 *Therefore . . . hands:* That is why I shook hands with all of you (because I intend to be counted as an ally of yours).

241 *Or else . . . spectacle:* If we could not give you reasons for what we have done, it would be nothing but an uncivilized show.

246-255 *That's all . . . utter:* Antony asks permission to carry Caesar's body outside and make a funeral speech in his honor. Brutus agrees, but Cassius fears that Antony's words might incite the people in Caesar's favor.

220 In terms of friendship with thine enemies.
Pardon me, Julius! Here wast thou bayed, brave hart;
Here didst thou fall; and here thy hunters stand,
Signed in thy spoil, and crimsoned in thy lethe.
O world, thou wast the forest to his hart;
225 And this indeed, O world, the heart of thee!
How like a deer, strucken by many princes,
Dost thou here lie!

Cassius. Mark Antony—

Antony.   Pardon me, Caius Cassius.
230 The enemies of Caesar shall say this;
Then, in a friend, it is cold modesty.

Cassius. I blame you not for praising Caesar so;
But what compact mean you have with us?
Will you be pricked in number of our friends,
235 Or shall we on, and not depend on you?

Antony. Therefore I took your hands; but was indeed
Swayed from the point by looking down on Caesar.
Friends am I with you all, and love you all,
Upon this hope, that you shall give me reasons
240 Why and wherein Caesar was dangerous.

Brutus. Or else were this a savage spectacle.
Our reasons are so full of good regard
That were you, Antony, the son of Caesar,
You should be satisfied.

245 **Antony.**   That's all I seek;
And am moreover suitor that I may
Produce his body to the market place
And in the pulpit, as becomes a friend,
Speak in the order of his funeral.

250 **Brutus.** You shall, Mark Antony.

Cassius. Brutus, a word with you.

[Aside to Brutus.]

259 *protest:* explain.

263 *It shall . . . wrong:* His speech will do us more good *(advantage more)* than harm.

277-298 Now that Antony is alone with Caesar's corpse, he speaks truthfully. His speech shows what he really thinks of the men who have just left and what he intends to do about the murder.

280 *in the tide of times:* in all of history.

You know not what you do. Do not consent.
That Antony speak in his funeral.
Know you how much the people may be moved
255   By that which he will utter?

Brutus. By your pardon,

[Aside to Cassius.]

I will myself into the pulpit first
And show the reason of our Caesar's death.
What Antony shall speak, I will protest
260   He speaks by leave and by permission,
And that we are contented Caesar shall
Have all true rites and lawful ceremonies.
It shall advantage more than do us wrong.

Cassius.

[Aside to Brutus.]

265   I know not what may fall. I like it not.

Brutus. Mark Antony, here, take you Caesar's body.
You shall not in your funeral speech blame us,
But speak all good you can devise of Caesar,
And say you do't by our permission.
270   Else shall you not have any hand at all
About his funeral. And you shall speak
In the same pulpit whereto I am going,
After my speech is ended.

Antony.   Be it so.
275   I do desire no more.

Brutus. Prepare the body then, and follow us.

[Exeunt all but Antony, who looks down at Caesar's body.]

Antony. O, pardon me, thou bleeding piece of earth,
That I am meek and gentle with these butchers!
Thou art the ruins of the noblest man
280   That ever lived in the tide of times.

286-292 *Domestic fury . . . deeds:* Rome *(Italy)* will be torn by civil war. People will become so accustomed to horrible sights that mothers will simply smile when they see their children cut into pieces *(quartered).* Pity will disappear among so much cruelty.

294 *Até (ā' tē):* the Greek goddess of revenge.

296 *"Havoc!":* a battle cry signaling mass killings.

298 *With carrion . . . burial:* like rotting corpses begging to be buried.

299 Antony is interrupted by a servant of Octavius, an ally of Caesar. The servant begins to relay a message, then sees the bleeding corpse on the floor.

309 *He lies . . . Rome:* Octavius will set up camp tonight about twenty-one miles *(seven leagues)* outside Rome.

310-321 *Post back . . . your hand:* Antony tells the servant to hurry back and tell Octavius what has happened. Then he tells the servant to wait. He wants the servant to listen to his funeral speech and report to Octavius how the crowd responds to it. *What do you think Antony's funeral speech will be like?*

Woe to the hand that shed this costly blood!
Over thy wounds now do I prophesy
(Which, like dumb mouths, do ope their ruby lips
To beg the voice and utterance of my tongue),
285 A curse shall light upon the limbs of men;
Domestic fury and fierce civil strife
Shall cumber all the parts of Italy;
Blood and destruction shall be so in use
And dreadful objects so familiar
290 That mothers shall but smile when they behold
Their infants quartered with the hands of war,
All pity choked with custom of fell deeds;
And Caesar's spirit, ranging for revenge,
With Até by his side come hot from hell,
295 Shall in these confines with a monarch's voice
Cry "Havoc!" and let slip the dogs of war,
That this foul deed shall smell above the earth
With carrion men, groaning for burial.

[Enter Octavius' Servant.]

You serve Octavius Caesar, do you not?

300 **Servant.** I do, Mark Antony.

Antony. Caesar did write for him to come to Rome.

Servant. He did receive his letters and is coming,
And bid me say to you by word of mouth—
O Caesar!

305 **Antony.** Thy heart is big. Get thee apart and weep.
Passion, I see, is catching, for mine eyes,
Seeing those beads of sorrow stand in thine,
Began to water. Is thy master coming?

Servant. He lies tonight within seven leagues of Rome.

310 **Antony.** Post back with speed and tell him what hath
chanced.
Here is a mourning Rome, a dangerous Rome,
No Rome of safety for Octavius yet.

2-8 ***give me audience:*** Listen to me. Brutus is shouting, trying to get the crowd to quiet down so he can speak. He asks Cassius to divide the crowd ***(part the numbers)*** and speak to another group. We will tell the people our reasons ***(public reasons shall be rendered)*** for killing Caesar, he says.

Hie hence and tell him so. Yet stay awhile.
315   Thou shalt not back till I have borne this corse
Into the market place. There shall I try
In my oration how the people take
The cruel issue of these bloody men,
According to the which thou shall discourse
320   To young Octavius of the state of things.
Lend me your hand.

[Exeunt with Caesar's *body.]*

Scene 2 *The Forum in Rome.*

*Brutus speaks before a group of "citizens," or
common people of Rome. He explains why
Caesar had to be slain for the good of Rome.
Then, Brutus leaves and Antony speaks to the
citizens. A far better judge of human nature
than Brutus, Antony cleverly manages to turn
the crowd against the conspirators by telling
them of Caesar's good works and his concern
for the people, as proven by the slain ruler's
will. He has left all his wealth to the people.
As Antony stirs the citizens to pursue the
assassins and kill them, he learns that Octavius
has arrived in Rome and that Brutus and
Cassius have fled.*

[Enter Brutus *and* Cassius *and a throng of* Citizens,
disturbed by the death of Caesar.*]*

Citizens. We will be satisfied! Let us be satisfied!

Brutus. Then follow me and give me audience, friends.
Cassius, go you into the other street
And part the numbers.
5   Those that will hear me speak, let 'em stay here;
Those that will follow Cassius, go with him;
And public reasons shall be rendered
Of Caesar's death.

14-40 As you read Brutus' speech, think about the kinds of
arguments he uses to persuade the crowd. *Does he try
to appeal to their emotions? Do you think he truly
believes that the killing was justified?*

14 *lovers:* friends.

17 *Censure me:* Judge me.

30-31 *Who is . . . bondman:* Which of you is so low that
you would prefer to be a slave?

32 *rude:* uncivilized.

37-40 *The question . . . death:* The reasons for his death
are on record in the Capitol. We have not belittled
(extenuated) his accomplishments or overemphasized
(enforced) the failings for which he was killed.

First Citizen. I will hear Brutus speak.

10 **Second Citizen.** I will hear Cassius, and compare their
reasons when severally we hear them rendered.

[Exit Cassius, *with some of the* Citizens. Brutus *goes into
the pulpit.]*

Third Citizen. The noble Brutus is ascended. Silence!

Brutus. Be patient till the last.
Romans, countrymen, and lovers, hear me for my
15 cause, and be silent, that you may hear. Believe me
for mine honor, and have respect to mine honor,
that you may believe. Censure me in your wisdom,
and awake your senses, that you may the better
judge. If there be any in this assembly, any dear
20 friend of Caesar's, to him I say that Brutus' love to
Caesar was no less than his. If then that friend
demand why Brutus rose against Caesar, this is my
answer: Not that I loved Caesar less, but that I loved
Rome more. Had you rather Caesar were living, and
25 die all slaves, than that Caesar were dead, to live all
freemen? As Caesar loved me, I weep for him; as he
was fortunate, I rejoice at it; as he was valiant, I
honor him; but—as he was ambitious, I slew him.
There is tears for his love; joy for his fortune; honor
30 for his valor; and death for his ambition. Who is
here so base that would be a bondman? If any,
speak, for him have I offended. Who is here so rude
that would not be a Roman? If any, speak, for him
have I offended. Who is here so vile that will not love
his country? If any, speak, for him have I offended. I
pause for a reply.

35 **All.** None, Brutus, none!

Brutus. Then none have I offended. I have done no
more to Caesar than you shall do to Brutus. The
question of his death is enrolled in the Capitol; his
glory not extenuated, wherein he was worthy, nor

48-58 *What is the mood of the crowd as Brutus finishes his speech?*

62 *grace his speech:* Listen to him respectfully.

66 *Save:* except.

67 *Is Brutus wise to depart before Antony makes his speech?*

68 *public chair:* speaker's platform.

40   his offenses enforced, for which he suffered death.

[Enter Antony and others, with Caesar's body.]
Here come his body, mourned by Mark Antony, who
though he had no hand in his death, shall receive
the benefit of his dying, a place in the common-
wealth, as which of you shall not? With this I depart,
45   that, as I slew my best lover for the good of Rome, I
have the same dagger for myself when it shall please
my country to need my death.

All. Live, Brutus! live, live!

First Citizen. Bring him with triumph home unto his
50   house.

Second Citizen. Give him a statue with his ancestors.

Third Citizen. Let him be Caesar.

Fourth Citizen.   Caesar's better parts
Shall be crowned in Brutus.

55 **First Citizen.** We'll bring him to his house with shouts
and clamors.

Brutus. My countrymen—

Second Citizen.   Peace! silence! Brutus speaks.

First Citizen. Peace ho!

60 **Brutus.** Good countrymen, let me depart alone,
And, for my sake, stay here with Antony.
Do grace to Caesar's corpse, and grace his speech
Tending to Caesar's glories which Mark Antony,
By our permission, is allowed to make.
65   I do entreat you, not a man depart,
Save I alone, till Antony have spoke.

[Exit]

First Citizen. Stay, ho! and let us hear Mark Antony.

Third Citizen. Let him go up into the public chair.

70 *beholding:* indebted.

71-78 Notice what the people are now saying about Caesar, only minutes after they were crying for him. Antony hears all this. *How do you think he will respond?*

82-149 Antony's words at Caesar's funeral make up one of the most famous speeches in all of Shakespeare's plays. Remember that Antony wants to stir the people into a civil war. He must work on them gradually, since they are now supporters of Brutus. One gradual change is in his use of the word *honorable.* As the speech goes on, the word becomes more and more sarcastic.

85 *interred:* buried.

84-86 *The evil . . . Caesar:* Let Caesar's good deeds die with him; let him be remembered by his faults.

88 *grievous:* serious.

90 *under leave of:* with the permission of.

95 *general coffers:* the Roman government's treasury.

We'll hear him. Noble Antony, go up.

70 **Antony.** For Brutus' sake I am beholding to you.

[Goes into the pulpit.]

Fourth Citizen. What does he say of Brutus?

Third Citizen. He says for Brutus' sake
He finds himself beholding to us all.

Fourth Citizen. 'Twere best he speak no harm of Brutus
75 here!

First Citizen. This Caesar was a tyrant.

Third Citizen. Nay, that's certain.
We are blest that Rome is rid of him.

Second Citizen. Peace! Let us hear what Antony can say.

80 **Antony.** You gentle Romans—

All. Peace, ho! Let us hear him.

Antony. Friends, Romans, countrymen, lend me your ears;
I come to bury Caesar, not to praise him.
The evil that men do lives after them;
85 The good is oft interred with their bones.
So let it be with Caesar. The noble Brutus
Hath told you Caesar was ambitious.
If it were so, it was a grievous fault,
And grievously hath Caesar answered it.
90 Here, under leave of Brutus and the rest
(For Brutus is an honorable man;
So are they all, all honorable men),
Come I to speak in Caesar's funeral.
He hath brought many captives home to Rome,
95 Whose ransoms did the general coffers fill.
Did this in Caesar seem ambitious?
When that the poor have cried, Caesar hath wept;
Ambition should be made of sterner stuff.
Yet Brutus says he was ambitious;

102 *thrice:* three times.

111-113 *Bear with . . . to me:* Antony stops speaking and
turns to the corpse. He says he is overcome with grief
(My heart is in the coffin) and needs to pause for a
while. *What other reasons might Antony have for
pausing at this point in his speech?*

123 *some will dear abide it:* Some will pay dearly for it.

130 *But:* only.

100 And Brutus is an honorable man.
You all did see that on the Lupercal
I thrice presented him a kingly crown,
Which he did thrice refuse. Was this ambition?
Yet Brutus says he was ambitious;
105 And sure he is an honorable man.
I speak not to disprove what Brutus spoke,
But here I am to speak what I do know.
You all did love him once, not without cause.
What cause withholds you then to mourn for him?
110 O judgment, thou art fled to brutish beasts,
And men have lost their reason! Bear with me,
My heart is in the coffin there with Caesar,
And I must pause till it come back to me.

First Citizen. Methinks there is much reason in his
115   sayings.

Second Citizen. If thou consider rightly of the matter,
Caesar has had great wrong.

Third Citizen.   Has he, masters?
I fear there will a worse come in his place.

120 **Fourth Citizen.** Marked ye his words? He would not take
the crown;
Therefore 'tis certain he was not ambitious.

First Citizen. If it be found so, some will dear abide it.

Second Citizen. Poor soul! his eyes are red as fire with
125   weeping.

Third Citizen. There's not a nobler man in Rome than
Antony.

Fourth Citizen. Now mark him. He begins again to
speak.

130 **Antony.** But yesterday the word of Caesar might
Have stood against the world. Now lies he there,
And none so poor to do him reverence.

136 *honorable men:* By this point, Antony is using the term more as an insult than a compliment. He spits it out angrily, wanting the crowd to know that he doesn't believe for a second that it describes the assassins.

140 *parchment:* document.

143 *Which . . . read:* Mark Antony is manipulating the crowd here. He has every intention of reading the will, but wants the crowd to force him to do so.

145 *napkins:* handkerchiefs.

148-149 *Bequeathing . . . issue:* People would leave it (a hair from Caesar's head) in their wills for their children *(issue).*

154 *meet:* proper.

163 *I have . . . of it:* I have gone too far in even mentioning it to you.

O masters! If I were disposed to stir
Your hearts and minds to mutiny and rage,
135 I should do Brutus wrong, and Cassius wrong,
Who, you all know, are honorable men.
I will not do them wrong. I rather choose
To wrong the dead, to wrong myself and you,
Than I will wrong such honorable men.
140 But here's a parchment with the seal of Caesar.
I found it in his closet; 'tis his will.
Let but the commons hear this testament,
Which (pardon me) I do not mean to read,
And they would go and kiss dead Caesar's wounds
145 And dip their napkins in his sacred blood;
Yea, beg a hair of him for memory,
And dying, mention it within their wills,
Bequeathing it as a rich legacy
Unto their issue.

150 **Fourth Citizen.** We'll hear the will! Read it, Mark
Antony.

All. The will, the will! We will hear Caesar's will!

Antony. Have patience, gentle friends, I must not read it.
It is not meet you know how Caesar loved you.
155 You are not wood, you are not stones, but men;
And being men, hearing the will of Caesar,
It will inflame you, it will make you mad.
'Tis good you know not that you are his heirs,
For if you should, O, what would come of it?

160 **Fourth Citizen.** Read the will! We'll hear it, Antony!
You shall read us the will, Caesar's will!

Antony. Will you be patient? Will you stay awhile?
I have o'ershot myself to tell you of it.
I fear I wrong the honorable men
165 Whose daggers have stabbed Caesar; I do fear it.

Fourth Citizen. They were traitors. Honorable men!

173 *Shall I . . . leave:* Will you give me permission to come down? Antony pretends to be at the mercy of the crowd. *Why do you think he does this?*

184 *mantle:* Caesar's toga.

187 *the Nervii:* a Belgian tribe that Caesar defeated thirteen years earlier.

189 *rent:* tear, hole.

192 *Mark:* notice.

193-194 *As rushing . . . or no:* Antony says Caesar's blood rushed out of that opening to find out if it really was Brutus who had made the wound.

All. The will! the testament!

Second Citizen. They were villains, murderers! The will!
Read the will!

170 **Antony.** You will compel me then to read the will?
Then make a ring about the corpse of Caesar
And let me show you him that made the will.
Shall I descend? and will you give me leave?

All. Come down.

175 **Second Citizen.** Descend.

Third Citizen. You shall have leave.

[Antony *comes down.*]

Fourth Citizen. A ring! Stand round.

First Citizen. Stand from the hearse! Stand from the
body!

180 **Second Citizen.** Room for Antony, most noble Antony!

Antony. Nay, press not so upon me. Stand far off.

All. Stand back! Room! Bear back!

Antony. If you have tears, prepare to shed them now.
You all do know this mantle. I remember
185 The first time ever Caesar put it on.
'Twas on a summer's evening in his tent,
That day he overcame the Nervii.
Look, in this place ran Cassius' dagger through.
See what a rent the envious Casca made.
190 Through this the well-beloved Brutus stabbed;
And as he plucked his cursed steel away,
Mark how the blood of Caesar followed it,
As rushing out of doors to be resolved
If Brutus so unkindly knocked or no;
195 For Brutus, as you know, was Caesar's angel.
Judge, O you gods, how dearly Caesar loved him!
This was the most unkindest cut of all;

200 *vanquished:* defeated.

208 *dint:* force.

209-211 *weep you . . . traitors:* Do you cry when you look only at his wounded clothing *(vesture)?* Here, look at his body! (Antony pulls Caesar's toga aside and reveals the knife wounds.) The people find the sight repulsive, and it makes them angry.

For when the noble Caesar saw him stab,
Ingratitude, more strong than traitors' arms,
200 Quite vanquishèd him. Then burst his mighty heart;
And in his mantle muffling up his face,
Even at the base of Pompey's statue
(Which all the while ran blood) great Caesar fell.
O, what a fall was there, my countrymen!
205 Then I, and you, and all of us fell down,
Whilst bloody treason flourished over us.
O, now you weep, and I perceive you feel
The dint of pity. These are gracious drops.
Kind souls, what, weep you when you but behold
210 Our Caesar's vesture wounded? Look you here!
Here is himself, marred, as you see, with traitors.

[Pulls the cloak off Caesar's body.]

First Citizen. O piteous spectacle!

Second Citizen. O noble Caesar!

Third Citizen. O woeful day!

215 **Fourth Citizen.** O traitors, villains!

First Citizen. O most bloody sight!

Second Citizen. We will be revenged.

All. Revenge! About! Seek! Burn! Fire! Kill! Slay!
Let not a traitor live!

220 **Antony.** Stay, countrymen.

First Citizen. Peace there! Hear the noble Antony.

Second Citizen. We'll hear him, we'll follow him,
we'll die with him!

Antony. Good friends, sweet friends, let me not stir you up
225 To such a sudden flood of mutiny.
They that have done this deed are honorable.
What private griefs they have, alas, I know not,
That made them do it. They are wise and honorable,

231-233 *I am no . . . friend:* This is another speaker's trick. Antony has just shown himself to be a much better speaker *(orator)* than Brutus. *Why, then, does he say he is "no orator"?*

235 *wit:* intelligence.

258 *drachmas:* silver coins, worth quite a bit to poor people such as those in the crowd.

And will no doubt with reasons answer you.
230 I come not, friends, to steal away your hearts.
I am no orator, as Brutus is,
But (as you know me all) a plain blunt man
That love my friend; and that they know full well
That gave me public leave to speak of him.
235 For I have neither wit, nor words, nor worth,
Action, nor utterance, nor the power of speech
To stir men's blood. I only speak right on.
I tell you that which you yourselves do know,
Show you sweet Caesar's wounds, poor poor dumb
240   mouths,
And bid them speak for me. But were I Brutus,
And Brutus Antony, there were an Antony
Would ruffle up your spirits, and put a tongue
In every wound of Caesar that should move
245 The stones of Rome to rise and mutiny.

All. We'll mutiny.

First Citizen.   We'll burn the house of Brutus.

Third Citizen. Away then! Come, seek the conspirators.

Antony. Yet hear me, countrymen. Yet hear me speak.

250 **All.** Peace, ho! Hear Antony, most noble Antony!

Antony. Why, friends, you go to do you know not what.
Wherein hath Caesar thus deserved your loves?
Alas, you know not! I must tell you then.
You have forgot the will I told you of.

255 **All.** Most true! The will! Let's stay and hear the will.

Antony. Here is the will, under Caesar's seal.
To every Roman citizen he gives,
To every several man, seventy-five drachmas.

Second Citizen. Most noble Caesar! We'll revenge his
260   death!

Third Citizen. O royal Caesar!

264-268 Reading from the will, Antony tells the crowd that Caesar has left all his private parks and gardens on this side of the Tiber River to be used by the public.

272 *brands:* pieces of burning wood.

277-278 *Now let . . . wilt:* Alone, Antony gloats over what he has just accomplished. Let things take their course, he says. Whatever happens, happens.

283 *thither . . . him:* I will go right there to see him.

284-285 *He comes . . . anything:* Octavius has arrived just as Antony hoped; Antony believes that Fortune, the goddess of fate, is on his side.

287 *Are rid:* have ridden.

288 *Belike:* probably.

Antony. Hear me with patience.

All. Peace, ho!

Antony. Moreover, he hath left you all his walks,
265   His private arbors, and new-planted orchards,
       On this side Tiber; he hath left them you,
       And to your heirs for ever—common pleasures,
       To walk abroad and recreate yourselves.
       Here was a Caesar! When comes such another?

270 **First Citizen.** Never, never! Come, away, away!
       We'll burn his body in the holy place
       And with the brands the traitors' houses.
       Take up the body.

Second Citizen. Go fetch fire!

275 **Third Citizen.** Pluck down benches!

Fourth Citizen. Pluck down forms, windows, anything!

[Exeunt Citizens with the body.]

Antony. Now let it work. Mischief, thou art afoot,
       Take thou what course thou wilt.

[Enter a Servant.]

                                    How now, fellow?

280 **Servant.** Sir, Octavius is already come to Rome.

Antony. Where is he?

Servant. He and Lepidus are at Caesar's house.

Antony. And thither will I straight to visit him.
       He comes upon a wish. Fortune is merry,
285   And in this mood will give us anything.

Servant. I heard him say Brutus and Cassius
       Are rid like madmen through the gates of Rome.

Antony. Belike they had some notice of the people,
       How I had moved them. Bring me to Octavius.

[Exeunt.]

2 *things . . . fantasy:* Recent events have caused me to imagine awful things.

6 *Whither:* where.

17-18 *That's . . . fear:* This response shows that Cinna is in danger. The citizen threatens to beat him **(*You'll bear me a bang*),** even though Cinna's comment was not meant to be insulting.

Scene 3 *A street in Rome.*

This scene involves a famous Roman poet named Cinna. (He is not the same Cinna who took part in the assassination.) The angry Roman mob comes upon the poet, believing he is Cinna the conspirator. Soon, they realize this is the wrong man, yet they are so enraged that they slay him anyway. Then, they rush through the city after the true killers of Caesar.

[Enter Cinna, *the* poet, *and after him the* Citizens, *armed with sticks, spears, and swords.]*

Cinna. I dreamt tonight that I did feast with Caesar,
And things unluckily charge my fantasy.
I have no will to wander forth of doors,
Yet something leads me forth.

5　**First Citizen.** What is your name?

Second Citizen. Whither are you going?

Third Citizen. Where do you dwell?

Fourth Citizen. Are you a married man or a bachelor?

Second Citizen. Answer every man directly.

10　**First Citizen.** Ay, and briefly.

Fourth Citizen. Ay, and wisely.

Third Citizen. Ay, and truly, you were best.

Cinna. What is my name? Whither am I going? Where
do I dwell? Am I a married man or a bachelor?
15　Then, to answer every man directly and briefly,
wisely and truly: wisely I say, I am a bachelor.

Second Citizen. That's as much to say they are fools
that marry. You'll bear me a bang for that, I fear.
Proceed—directly.

20　**Cinna.** Directly I am going to Caesar's funeral.

34-35 ***Pluck . . . going:*** Let's just tear the name out of his heart and send him away.

36 The citizens murder Cinna the poet. *Can you think of other examples—from real life or literature—of crowds that have gotten out of control?*

First Citizen. As a friend or an enemy?

Cinna. As a friend.

Second Citizen. That matter is answered directly.

Fourth Citizen. For your dwelling—briefly.

25 **Cinna.** Briefly, I dwell by the Capitol.

Third Citizen. Your name, sir, truly.

Cinna. Truly, my name is Cinna.

First Citizen. Tear him to pieces! He's a conspirator.

Cinna. I am Cinna the poet! I am Cinna the poet!

30 **Fourth Citizen.** Tear him for his bad verses! Tear him
for his bad verses!

Cinna. I am not Cinna the conspirator.

Fourth Citizen. It is no matter; his name's Cinna!
Pluck but his name out of his heart, and turn him
35 going.

Third Citizen. Tear him, tear him!

[They attack Cinna.]
Come, brands, ho! To Brutus', to Cassius'! Burn all!
Some to Decius' house and some to Casca's; some to
Ligarius'! Away, go!

[Exeunt all the citizens.]

9 **with a spot . . . him:** I condemn him by marking him
on this list.

11-12 **Fetch . . . legacies:** Bring Caesar's will here, so we can
decide how to alter the amounts the people get. *Does
this statement change your opinion of Antony?
Explain.*

FOUR

Scene 1 *At a table in Antony's house in Rome.*

*Antony, Octavius, and Lepidus now rule Rome
as a triumvirate—a committee of three. The
scene opens on the triumvirate, meeting to
draw up a list of their enemies who must be
killed. They also discuss changing Caesar's will.
As Lepidus goes to fetch the will, Antony
expresses his low opinion of Lepidus as a
leader. Then, Antony and Octavius begin to
discuss how to defeat the armies of Brutus
and Cassius.*

Antony. These many, then, shall die; their names are
    pricked.

Octavius. Your brother too must die. Consent you,
    Lepidus?

5 **Lepidus.** I do consent.

Octavius.   Prick him down, Anthony.

Lepidus. Upon condition Publius shall not live,
    Who is your sister's son, Mark Antony.

Antony. He shall not live. Look, with a spot I damn him.
10   But Lepidus, go you to Caesar's house.
    Fetch the will hither, and we shall determine
    How to cut off some charge in legacies.

Lepidus. What? shall I find you here?

Octavius. Or here or at the Capitol.

[Exit Lepidus.]

15-31 *This is . . . commons:* Now that Antony and Octavius are alone, Antony says what he really thinks of Lepidus. He does not believe Lepidus is worthy of being one of three men in control of Rome's lands in Europe, Asia, and Africa *(the threefold world).* Lepidus, he says, is fit *(Meet)* for running errands. Antony admits that they have accepted Lepidus' opinion about who should be put on the list of those who will die *(black sentence and proscription),* but they have done that only so he will take the blame for the many unpopular things *(divers sland'rous loads)* they plan to do.

34-35 *So is my . . . property:* Antony compares Lepidus to a horse who is given food *(provender)* and taught how to behave. Antony also says that Lepidus is interested in *(feeds / On)* unimportant things *(objects, arts, and imitations)* that he learns of from other people, and these things attract his attention *(Begin his fashion)* after others have lost interest in them.

46-47 *Listen . . . head:* Listen to important *(great)* matters. Brutus and Cassius are raising an army *(levying powers).* We must move fast *(straight make head)* to build up our own army.

15 **Antony.** This is a slight unmeritable man,
Meet to be sent on errands. Is it fit,
The threefold world divided, he should stand
One of the three to share it?

Octavius.   So you thought him,
20 And took his voice who should be pricked to die
In our black sentence and proscription.

Antony. Octavius, I have seen more days than you;
And though we lay these honors on this man
To ease ourselves of divers sland'rous loads,
25 He shall but bear them as the ass bears gold,
To groan and sweat under the business,
Either led or driven as we point the way;
And having brought our treasure where we will,
Then take we down his load, and turn him off
30 (Like to the empty ass) to shake his ears
And graze in commons.

Octavius.   You may do your will;
But he's a tried and valiant soldier.

Antony. So is my horse, Octavius, and for that
35 I do appoint him store of provender.
It is a creature that I teach to fight,
To wind, to stop, to run directly on,
His corporal motion governed by my spirit.
And, in some taste is Lepidus but so.
40 He must be taught, and trained, and bid go forth:
A barren-spirited fellow; one that feeds
On objects, arts and imitations
Which, out of use and staled by other men,
Begin his fashion. Do not talk of him,
45 But as a property. And now, Octavius,
Listen great things. Brutus and Cassius
Are levying powers. We must straight make head.
Therefore let our alliance be combined,
Our best friends made, and our best means stretched
50   out;

51-53 *let us . . . answered:* Let us decide the best way to uncover hidden *(covert)* dangers and to deal with the threats we know about.

54-57 *for we are . . . mischiefs:* We are like a bear tied to a stake and taunted by barking dogs. Some of the people who smile at us may have evil intentions *(mischiefs)* in mind for us. *What do these lines tell you about Octavius' state of mind?*

5 *do you salutation:* bring you greetings.

6-10 *He greets . . . satisfied:* Cassius sends a good man to greet me. Pindarus, your master has either had a change of heart or is surrounded by incompetent *(ill)* officers. Whatever the reason, he has made me wish that certain things had never happened *(Things done undone).* But if he is here *(at hand),* I will find out for myself *(be satisfied).*

And let us presently go sit in council
How covert matters may be best disclosed
And open perils surest answered.

Octavius. Let us do so; for we are at the stake
55   And bayed about with many enemies;
And some that smile have in their hearts, I fear,
Millions of mischiefs.

[Exeunt.]

Scene 2 *A military camp near Sardis. In front of Brutus' tent.*

*Brutus seems displeased at the way events are
developing, and he tells his servant about
Cassius' new cold and distant attitude. Cassius
arrives, and he and Brutus go into the tent to
talk about their disagreements.*

[Sound of drums. Enter Brutus, Lucilius, Lucius, *and*
Soldiers. Titinius *and* Pindarus, *from* Cassius' *army,
meet them.]*

Brutus. Stand ho!

Lucilius. Give the word, ho! and stand!

Brutus. What now, Lucilius? Is Cassius near?

Lucilius. He is at hand, and Pindarus is come
5   To do you salutation from his master.

Brutus. He greets me well. Your master, Pindarus,
In his own change, or by ill officers,
Hath given me some worthy cause to wish
Things done undone; but if he be at hand,
10   I shall be satisfied.

Pindarus.   I do not doubt
But that my noble master will appear
Such as he is, full of regard and honor.

14-15 ***A word . . . resolved:*** Brutus takes his officer aside and asks him privately how he was treated when he met Cassius. *Why does Brutus want to know this?*

18 ***conference:*** conversation.

21-29 ***Ever note . . . trial:*** Brutus tells Lucilius never to forget ***(Ever note)*** that when affection begins to cool, it turns into awkward politeness ***(enforced ceremony).*** Honest relationships, he says, do not involve tricks. Insincere ***(hollow)*** men, like eager horses, make a great show of courage ***(mettle).*** But when they get the signal ***(spur)*** to fight, they drop their heads ***(fall their crests)*** and fail, like worn-out horses ***(jades).***

30 ***They . . . quartered:*** Cassius and his army intend to stay here (in Sardis) tonight.

31 ***horse in general:*** entire cavalry.

37-39 The soldiers are passing the order to stop marching ***(Stand)*** along the lengthy column that has followed Cassius into camp.

Brutus. He is not doubted. A word, Lucilius,
15   How he received you. Let me be resolved.

Lucilius. With courtesy and with respect enough,
     But not with such familiar instances
     Nor with such free and friendly conference
     As he hath used of old.

20 **Brutus.**   Thou has described
     A hot friend cooling. Ever note, Lucilius,
     When love begins to sicken and decay
     It useth an enforced ceremony.
     There are no tricks in plain and simple faith;
25   But hollow men, like horses hot at hand,
     Make gallant show and promise of their mettle;

[Low march within.]

     But when they should endure the bloody spur,
     They fall their crests, and like deceitful jades
     Sink in the trial. Comes his army on?

30 **Lucilius.** They mean this night in Sardis to be quartered.
     The greater part, the horse in general,
     Are come with Cassius.

Brutus.   Hark! He is arrived.
     March gently on to meet him.

[Enter Cassius and his army.]

35 **Cassius.** Stand, ho!

Brutus. Stand, ho! Speak the word along.

First Soldier. Stand!

Second Soldier. Stand!

Third Soldier. Stand!

40 **Cassius.** Most noble brother, you have done me wrong.

Brutus. Judge me, you gods! wrong I mine enemies?
     And if not so, how should I wrong a brother?

43 *sober form:* serious manner.

45-51 *be content . . . audience:* Brutus tells Cassius to stay calm and keep his voice down. He says they should not argue *(wrangle)* in front of their soldiers. Then he invites Cassius into his tent, where he will listen to him *(give you audience). Why does Brutus want to hide his and Cassius' disagreements from the soldiers?*

2 *noted:* publicly disgraced.

Cassius. Brutus, this sober form of yours hides wrongs,
And when you do them—

45 **Brutus.**   Cassius, be content.
Speak your griefs softly. I do know you well.
Before the eyes of both our armies here
(Which should perceive nothing but love from us)
Let us not wrangle. Bid them move away.
50 Then in my tent, Cassius, enlarge your griefs,
And I will give you audience.

Cassius.   Pindarus,
Bid our commanders lead their charges off
A little from this ground.

55 **Brutus.** Lucilius, do you the like, and let no man
Come to our tent till we have done our conference.
Let Lucius and Titinius guard our door.

[Exeunt.]

Scene 3 *Inside Brutus' tent at Sardis.*

*Brutus and Cassius argue angrily, as Brutus
accuses Cassius of corruption and greed. After a
while, though, they calm down and become
friendly once again. Brutus informs Cassius of
Portia's death. Soon after, Massala enters. He tells
of all the killings in Rome and of Antony and
Octavius approaching with their armies. Brutus
persuades Cassius that their forces must meet the
enemy at Philippi in Greece. Later, as Brutus reads,
the ghost of Caesar appears and promises to see
Brutus at Philippi.*

[Enter Brutus and Cassius.]

Cassius. That you have wronged me doth appear in this:
You have condemned and noted Lucius Pella
For taking bribes here of the Sardians;
Wherein my letters, praying on his side,

5 *slighted off:* ignored.

7-8 *it is not . . . comment:* It is not appropriate for every tiny *(nice)* offense to be criticized.

10 *to have an itching palm:* to be always looking for bribes.

11 *mart:* market.

13-15 *I an . . . last:* Cassius is almost speechless at the insult Brutus has just hurled at him. If anyone other than Brutus said such a thing to me, Cassius says, I would kill him on the spot.

16-17 *The name . . . head:* Because Cassius' name is linked to the bribery *(corruption),* no one dares talk about punishment *(chastisement)* for those who accept the bribes.

24 *But for supporting robbers:* because he (Caesar) protected robbers from punishment. This is not one of the charges the conspirators originally made against Caesar.

28 *bay:* howl at.

30-34 *bait not me . . . conditions:* Do not try to provoke *(bait)* me into fighting. I will not put up with *(endure)* it. Since I am the more experienced soldier, I should be the one to make decisions *(conditions).*

5 Because I knew the man, were slighted off.

Brutus. You wronged yourself to write in such a case.

Cassius. In such a time as this it is not meet
That every nice offense should bear his comment.

Brutus. Let me tell you, Cassius, you yourself
10 Are much condemned to have an itching palm,
To sell and mart your offices for gold
To undeservers.

Cassius.   I an itching palm?
You know that you are Brutus that speaks this,
15 Or, by the gods, this speech were else your last!

Brutus. The name of Cassius honors this corruption,
And chastisement doth therefore hide his head.

Cassius. Chastisement?

Brutus. Remember March; the ides of March remember.
20 Did not great Julius bleed for justice' sake?
What villain touched his body that did stab
And not for justice? What, shall one of us,
That struck the foremost man of all this world
But for supporting robbers—shall we now
25 Contaminate our fingers with base bribes,
And sell the mighty space of our large honors
For so much trash as may be grasped thus?
I had rather be a dog and bay the moon
Than such a Roman.

30 **Cassius.**   Brutus, bait not me!
I'll not endure it. You forget yourself
To hedge me in. I am a soldier, I,
Older in practice, abler than yourself
To make conditions.

35 **Brutus.**   Go to! You are not, Cassius.

Cassius. I am.

Brutus. I say you are not.

43-52 **Must . . . spleen:** Brutus refers to Cassius' quick temper **(rash choler),** to the fact that he is so angry **(choleric),** and to his irritable mood **(testy humor).** You can swallow the poison of your own anger **(spleen),** he says. (People once believed that the spleen, an organ near the stomach, was the source of certain emotions, such as anger and spite.)

55 **waspish:** ill tempered.

58 **vaunting:** bragging; *What challenge does Brutus make?*

61-63 **You wrong . . . better:** Cassius now controls his anger and tries to soften some of the things he said earlier. He will soon become angry again, though, since Brutus does not stop insulting him.

66-67 **he durst . . . me:** Even Caesar would not have dared to provoke me this way.

Cassius. Urge me no more! I shall forget myself.
Have mind upon your health, tempt me no farther.

40 **Brutus.** Away, slight man!

Cassius. Is't possible?

Brutus.   Hear me, for I will speak.
Must I give way and room to your rash choler?
Shall I be frighted when a madman stares?

45 **Cassius.** O ye gods, ye gods! Must I endure all this?

Brutus. All this? Ay, more! Fret till your proud heart
break.
Go show your slaves how choleric you are
And make your bondmen tremble. Must I budge?
50 Must I observe you? Must I stand and crouch
Under your testy humor? By the gods,
You shall digest the venom of your spleen,
Though it do split you; for from this day forth
I'll use you for my mirth, yea, for my laughter,
55 When you are waspish.

Cassius.   Is it come to this?

Brutus. You say you are a better soldier;
Let it appear so. Make your vaunting true,
And it shall please me well. For mine own part,
60 I shall be glad to learn of noble men.

Cassius. You wrong me every way! You wrong me,
Brutus!
I said an elder soldier, not a better.
Did I say "better"?

65 **Brutus.** If you did, I care not.

Cassius. When Caesar lived he durst not thus have
moved me.

Brutus. Peace, peace! You durst not so have tempted
him.

82-86 *For I can . . . indirection:* I cannot raise money by dishonest *(vile)* methods. I would rather make coins out of my heart and blood than steal money from peasants by lying *(indirection)*.

87 *legions:* armies.

89-93 *Should . . . pieces:* Would I have answered a request from you in the same way? When I become such a miser *(so covetous)* as to deny cheap coins *(rascal counters)* to my friends, may the gods destroy me.

97 *rived:* torn apart.

98 *infirmities:* shortcomings.

70 **Cassius.** I durst not?

Brutus. No.

Cassius. What, durst not tempt him?

Brutus. For your life you durst not.

Cassius. Do not presume too much upon my love.
75   I may do that I shall be sorry for.

Brutus. You have done that you should be sorry for.
    There is no terror, Cassius, in your threats;
    For I am armed so strong in honesty
    That they pass by me as the idle wind,
80   Which I respect not. I did send to you
    For certain sums of gold, which you denied me,
    For I can raise no money by vile means—
    By heaven, I had rather coin my heart
    And drop my blood for drachmas than to wring
85   From the hard hands of peasants their vile trash
    By any indirection. I did send
    To you for gold to pay my legions,
    Which you denied me. Was that done like Cassius?
    Should I have answered Caius Cassius so?
90   When Marcus Brutus grows so covetous
    To lock such rascal counters from his friends,
    Be ready, gods, with all your thunderbolts,
    Dash him to pieces!

Cassius. I denied you not.

95 **Brutus.** You did.

Cassius. I did not. He was but a fool that brought
    My answer back. Brutus hath rived my heart.
    A friend should bear his friend's infirmities,
    But Brutus makes mine greater than they are.

100 **Brutus.** I do not, till you practice them on me.

Cassius. You love me not.

Brutus. I do not like your faults.

106-121 ***Come . . . lov'dst Cassius:*** Cassius speaks these lines loudly, as though calling to Antony and Octavius, who are far away. He says they might as well kill him. He has been bullied ***(braved)*** by his true friend ***(brother)*** and scolded ***(Checked)*** like a slave; his faults have been written in a notebook and memorized ***(conned by rote)*** to be thrown into his face ***(cast into my teeth).*** Cassius then turns to Brutus and offers Cassius' knife to plunge into his own heart.

122-128 ***Sheathe . . . cold again:*** Put away ***(Sheathe)*** your knife. Let your anger run free ***(have scope).*** Your insults ***(dishonor)*** will be taken as coming from a bad mood ***(humor).*** Cassius, you are tied to ***(yoked with)*** a mild man ***(lamb);*** anger to me is like the flint to fire. Strike it hard, and it will produce sparks; then it will cool immediately.

129-131 ***Hath Cassius . . . him:*** Have I lived so long only to become a joke to you when sadness and sickness trouble ***(vexeth)*** you?

134 The two men embrace in friendship, glad to be over their anger with each other.

Cassius. A friendly eye could never see such faults.

Brutus. A flatterer's would not, though they do appear
105   As huge as high Olympus.

Cassius. Come, Antony, and young Octavius, come!
    Revenge yourselves alone on Cassius.
    For Cassius is aweary of the world:
    Hated by one he loves; braved by his brother;
110   Checked like a bondman, all his faults observed,
    Set in a notebook, learned and conned by rote
    To cast into my teeth. O, I could weep
    My spirit from mine eyes! There is my dagger,
    And here my naked breast; within, a heart
115   Dearer than Pluto's mine, richer than gold:
    If that thou be'st a Roman, take it forth.
    I, that denied thee gold, will give my heart.
    Strike as thou didst at Caesar; for I know,
    When thou didst hate him worst, thou lov'dst him
120   better
    Than ever thou lov'dst Cassius.

Brutus.   Sheathe your dagger.
    Be angry when you will; it shall have scope.
    Do what you will; dishonor shall be humor.
125   O Cassius, you are yoked with a lamb
    That carries anger as the flint bears fire;
    Who, much enforced, shows a hasty spark,
    And straight is cold again.

Cassius.   Hath Cassius lived
130   To be but mirth and laughter to his Brutus
    When grief and blood ill-tempered vexeth him?

Brutus. When I spoke that, I was ill-tempered too.

Cassius. Do you confess so much? Give me your hand.

Brutus. And my heart too.

135 **Cassius.**   O Brutus!

Brutus.   What's the matter?

137-139 ***Have you . . . forgetful:*** Don't you love me enough to put up with me when I lose control because of that bad temper I inherited from my mother?

142 ***He'll think . . . so:*** I will say it is your mother, not you, showing bad temper, and will forget about it. *Do you find Shakespeare's portrayal of this argument and its ending believable? Explain.*

143-158 The two men are briefly interrupted by a poet, who comes to persuade them to end their arguments and insists that nothing will stop ***(stay)*** him. These lines show that the tension between Brutus and Cassius is now completely gone. They joke about what a terrible poet this rude fellow ***(cynic)*** is and finally send him away. Once the silly poet is gone, Brutus and Cassius— friends once again—become serious.

Cassius. Have you not love enough to bear with me
    When that rash humor which my mother gave me
    Makes me forgetful?

140 **Brutus.**   Yes, Cassius, and from henceforth,
    When you are over-earnest with your Brutus,
    He'll think your mother chides, and leave you so.

[Enter a Poet *followed by* Lucilius, Titinius, *and* Lucius.*]*

Poet. Let me go in to see the generals!
    There is some grudge between 'em. 'Tis not meet
145   They be alone.

Lucilius. You shall not come to them.

Poet. Nothing but death shall stay me.

Cassius. How now? What's the matter?

Poet. For shame, you generals! What do you mean?
150   Love and be friends, as two such men should be,
    For I have seen more years, I'm sure, than ye.

Cassius. Ha, ha! How vilely doth this cynic rhyme!

Brutus. Get you hence, sirrah! Saucy fellow, hence!

Cassius. Bear with him, Brutus. 'Tis his fashion.

155 **Brutus.** I'll know his humor when he knows his time.
    What should the wars do with these jigging fools?
    Companion, hence!

Cassius.   Away, away, be gone!

[Exit Poet.]

Brutus. Lucilius and Titinius, bid the commanders
160   Prepare to lodge their companies tonight.

Cassius. And come yourselves, and bring Messala with
    you
    Immediately to us.

[Exeunt Lucilius and Titinius.]

167-168 *Of your . . . evils:* You aren't making use of your philosophy if you let chance happenings get you down. (Brutus was a Stoic, one who believed that pain and suffering should be endured calmly and that self-control was all-important.)

170 *Ha:* Cassius is not laughing but is so shocked by the news of Portia's death that he gasps.

172 *How . . . so?* How did I escape being killed when I angered you, with such a terrible thing on your mind?

175-179 *Impatient . . . fire:* She was worried about my absence and about the armies of Antony and Octavius. These things made her depressed *(she fell distract).* When her servants were not around, she swallowed a hot coal and choked.

186 *o'erswell:* overflow.

Brutus.   Lucius, a bowl of wine.

[Exit Lucius.]

165 **Cassius.** I did not think you could have been so angry.

Brutus. O Cassius, I am sick of many griefs.

Cassius. Of your philosophy you make no use
   If you give place to accidental evils.

Brutus. No man bears sorrow better. Portia is dead.

170 **Cassius.** Ha! Portia?

Brutus. She is dead.

Cassius. How scaped I killing when I crossed you so?
   O insupportable and touching loss!
   Upon what sickness?

175 **Brutus.**   Impatient of my absence,
   And grief that young Octavius with Mark Antony
   Have made themselves so strong—for with her death
   That tidings came—with this she fell distract,
   And (her attendants absent) swallowed fire.

180 **Cassius.** And died so?

Brutus.   Even so.

Cassius. O ye immortal gods!

[Reenter Lucius, with wine and tapers.]

Brutus. Speak no more of her. Give me a bowl of wine.
   In this I bury all unkindness, Cassius.

[Drinks.]

185 **Cassius.** My heart is thirsty for that noble pledge.
   Fill, Lucius, till the wine o'erswell the cup.
   I cannot drink too much of Brutus' love.

[Drinks. Exit Lucius.]

[Reenter Titinius, with Messala.]

189-190 *Now sit . . . necessities:* Let's sit around this candle and talk about what we must do.

191-193 Cassius is distracted from the business that has to be discussed. He is having trouble believing that Portia is dead. Brutus asks him to stop talking about the painful topic.

196 *Bending . . . Philippi:* leading their armies to Philippi (a city in northern Greece).

197 *Myself . . . tenure:* I have received letters that say the same thing.

199 *proscription . . . outlawry:* official statements that declare certain acts to be criminal.

Brutus. Come in, Titinius! Welcome, good Messala.
Now sit we close about this taper here
190 And call in question our necessities.

Cassius. Portia, art thou gone?

Brutus.   No more, I pray you.
Messala, I have here received letters
That young Octavius and Mark Antony
195 Come down upon us with a mighty power,
Bending their expedition toward Philippi.

Messala. Myself have letters of the selfsame tenure.

Brutus. With what addition?

Messala. That by proscription and bills of outlawry
200 Octavius, Antony, and Lepidus
Have put to death an hundred senators.

Brutus. Therein our letters do not well agree.
Mine speak of seventy senators that died
By their proscriptions, Cicero being one.

205 **Cassius.** Cicero one?

Messala.   Cicero is dead,
And by that order of proscription.
Had you your letters from your wife, my lord?

Brutus. No, Messala.

210 **Messala.** Nor nothing in your letters writ of her?

Brutus. Nothing, Messala.

Messala.   That methinks is strange.

Brutus. Why ask you? Hear you aught of her in yours?

Messala. No, my lord.

215 **Brutus.** Now as you are a Roman, tell me true.

Messala. Then like a Roman bear the truth I tell,
For certain she is dead, and by strange manner.

222 ***in art:*** in theory, in my beliefs.

229-232 *How would you rephrase Cassius' reasons for not wanting to attack the armies of Antony and Octavius?*

233-242 ***Good . . . our back:*** Good reasons have to give way to better ones. The people between ***('twixt)*** here and Philippi are friendly only because they have to be ***(stand but in a forced affection).*** They have given us aid grudgingly. If the enemy marches through, they will find recruits. If we face them at Philippi, we'll eliminate this advantage and keep these unfriendly people behind us.

244-248 ***Under . . . decline:*** Brutus cuts Cassius off and insists on his own position. Their army, he says, is as good as it is ever going to get, while the enemy is getting stronger every day. *Do you agree with Brutus or Cassius? Why?*

245 ***tried the utmost:*** received all we can expect.

249-255 ***There is . . . ventures:*** Brutus compares life to a voyage on a ship. Following the high tide can lead to good fortune. Those who do not follow the tide might spend the rest of their lives in shallow water and misery. Our tide comes now, he insists, and we must act now.

Brutus. Why, farewell, Portia. We must die, Messala.
　　With meditating that she must die once,
220　　I have the patience to endure it now.

Messala. Even so great men great losses should endure.

Cassius. I have as much of this in art as you,
　　But yet my nature could not bear it so.

Brutus. Well, to our work alive. What do you think
225　　Of marching to Philippi presently?

Cassius. I do not think it good.

Brutus. 　　　　　　　　　　　　Your reason?

Cassius. 　　　　　　　　　　　　　　　This it is:
　　'Tis better that the enemy seek us.
230　　So shall he waste his means, weary his soldiers,
　　Doing himself offense, whilst we, lying still,
　　Are full of rest, defense, and nimbleness.

Brutus. Good reasons must of force give place to better.
　　The people 'twixt Philippi and this ground
235　　Do stand but in a forced affection,
　　For they have grudged us contribution.
　　The enemy, marching along by them,
　　By them shall make a fuller number up,
　　Come on refreshed, new-added, and encouraged;
240　　From which advantage we cut him off
　　If at Philippi we do face him there,
　　These people at our back.

Cassius. 　　　　　　　　　　Hear me, good brother.

Brutus. Under your pardon. You must note beside
245　　That we have tried the utmost of our friends,
　　Our legions are brimful, our cause is ripe.
　　The enemy increaseth every day;
　　We, at the height, are ready to decline.
　　There is a tide in the affairs of men
250　　Which, taken at the flood, leads on to fortune;

260 *Which . . . rest:* We will reluctantly satisfy *(niggard)* nature by getting a little bit of rest.

265 *gown:* nightgown.

Omitted, all the voyage of their life
Is bound in shallows and in miseries.
On such a full sea are we now afloat,
And we must take the current when it serves
255   Or lose our ventures.

Cassius.   Then, with your will, go on.
We'll along ourselves and meet them at Philippi.

Brutus. The deep of night is crept upon our talk
And nature must obey necessity,
260   Which we will niggard with a little rest.
There is no more to say?

Cassius.   No more. Good night.
Early tomorrow will we rise and hence.

Brutus. Lucius!

[Reenter Lucius.]

265   My gown.

[Exit Lucius.]

Farewell, good Messala.
Good night, Titinius. Noble, noble Cassius,
Good night and good repose!

Cassius.   O my dear brother,

270   This was an ill beginning of the night!
Never come such division 'tween our souls!
Let it not, Brutus.

[Reenter Lucius, with the gown.]

Brutus.   Everything is well.

Cassius. Good night, my lord.

275   **Brutus.**   Good night, good brother.

Titinius and Messala. Good night, Lord Brutus.

Brutus.   Farewell every one.

278 ***Where is thy instrument?*** One of Lucius' duties as a personal servant is to play music that will help Brutus get to sleep.

280-281 ***What . . . o'erwatched:*** I see you're sleepy. It's no wonder, since you've been watching and waiting for so long.

287-292 ***It may . . . bethink me:*** Brutus wants them to be handy in case he needs to send a message to Cassius. Varro offers to stand guard all night. Brutus insists the men sleep, not stand guard. He says he may change his mind ***(otherwise bethink me)*** about sending messages to Cassius.

[Exeunt all but Brutus *and* Lucius.*]*

Give me the gown. Where is thy instrument?

Lucius. Here in the tent.

280 **Brutus.**   What, thou speak'st drowsily?
Poor knave, I blame thee not, thou art o'erwatched.
Call Claudius and some other of my men;
I'll have them sleep on cushions in my tent.

Lucius. Varro and Claudius!

[Enter Varro *and* Claudius.*]*

285 **Varro.** Calls my lord?

Brutus. I pray you, sirs, lie in my tent and sleep.
It may be I shall raise you by-and-by
On business to my brother Cassius.

Varro. So please you, we will stand and watch your
290   pleasure.

Brutus. I will not have it so. Lie down, good sirs.
It may be I shall otherwise bethink me.

*[*Varro *and* Claudius *lie down.]*

Look, Lucius, here's the book I sought for so;
I put it in the pocket of my gown.

295 **Lucius.** I was sure your lordship did not give it me.

Brutus. Bear with me, good boy, I am much forgetful.
Canst thou hold up by thy heavy eyes awhile,
And touch thy instrument a strain or two?

Lucius. Ay, my lord, an't please you.

300 **Brutus.**   It does, my boy.
I trouble thee too much, but thou art willing.

Lucius. It is my duty, sir.

Brutus. I should not urge thy duty past thy might.

310 *mace:* a rod used as a symbol of authority. Brutus is addressing slumber as though it were an officer of the law who has arrested Lucius.

317 *How . . . burns:* How poorly this candle burns. Everyone in the tent is asleep, except Brutus. At first he thinks the thing he sees is only the result of poor eyesight. Then he realizes that something is really there.

I know young bloods look for a time of rest.

305 **Lucius.** I have slept, my lord, already.

Brutus. It was well done; and thou shalt sleep again;
I will not hold thee long. If I do live,
I will be good to thee.

[Music, and a song. Lucius falls asleep as he sings.]

This is a sleepy tune. O murd'rous slumber!
310 Layest thou thy leaden mace upon my boy,
That plays thee music? Gentle knave, good night.
I will not do thee so much wrong to wake thee.
If thou dost nod, thou break'st thy instrument;
I'll take it from thee; and, good boy, good night.
315 Let me see, let me see. Is not the leaf turned down
Where I left reading? Here it is, I think.

[Sits.]

[Enter the Ghost of Caesar.]

How ill this taper burns! Ha! Who comes here?
I think it is the weakness of mine eyes
That shapes this monstrous apparition.
320 It comes upon me. Art thou anything?
Art thou some god, some angel, or some devil,
That mak'st my blood cold and my hair to stare?
Speak to me what thou art.

Ghost. Thy evil spirit, Brutus.

325 **Brutus.**   Why com'st thou?

Ghost. To tell thee thou shalt see me at Philippi.

Brutus. Well; then I shall see thee again?

Ghost. Ay, at Philippi.

Brutus. Why, I will see thee at Philippi then.

[Exit Ghost.]

330 ***Now . . . vanishest:*** Now that I have my courage
back, you disappear. *What might have been
Shakespeare's purpose in adding a ghost to this play?*

334 ***false:*** out of tune, Lucius, only half awake, thinks he is
playing the instrument that Brutus took from him
earlier. *Why does Brutus accuse Lucius, Claudius, and
Varro of crying out in their sleep?*

352 ***commend me:*** give my respects to.

353 ***Bid . . . before:*** Tell him to get his army ***(pow'rs)***
moving early in the morning.

330   Now I have taken heart thou vanishest.
        Ill spirit, I would hold more talk with thee.
        Boy! Lucius! Varro! Claudius! Sirs! Awake!
        Claudius!

Lucius. The strings, my lord, are false.

335 **Brutus.** He thinks he still is at his instrument.
        Lucius, awake!

Lucius. My lord?

Brutus. Didst thou dream, Lucius, that thou so criedst
        out?

340 **Lucius.** My lord, I do not know that I did cry.

Brutus. Yes, that thou didst. Didst thou see anything?

Lucius. Nothing, my lord.

Brutus. Sleep again, Lucius. Sirrah Claudius!

[To Varro]

Fellow thou, awake!

345 **Varro.** My lord?

Claudius. My lord?

Brutus. Why did you so cry out, sirs, in your sleep?

Both. Did we, my lord?

Brutus.   Ay. Saw you anything?

350 **Varro.** No, my lord, I saw nothing.

Claudius.   Nor I, my lord.

Brutus. Go and commend me to my brother Cassius.
        Bid him set on his powers betimes before,
        And we will follow.

355 **Both.**   It shall be done, my lord.

[Exeunt.]

3 *keep . . . regions:* stay in the higher areas (where they could defend themselves more easily).

5 *warn:* challenge.

7-11 *I am . . . courage:* I know their secrets *(am in their bosoms)* and why they have done this. They would rather be in other places, not here fighting us. They come down with a show of bravery, thinking they will convince us they have courage.

15 *sign of battle:* a red flag symbolizing readiness for battle.

17-21 Antony and Octavius have a small argument about whose soldiers will fight on each side of the field. *Who wins this argument?*

FIVE

Scene 1 *The plains of Philippi in Greece.*

Antony and Octavius enter the battlefield with their army. Brutus and Cassius enter with their forces. The four leaders meet, but they only exchange insults and taunts. Antony and Octavius leave to prepare for battle. Cassius expresses his fears to Messala. Finally, Brutus and Cassius say their final farewells, in case they should die in battle.

[Enter Octavius, Antony, and their Army.]

Octavius. Now Antony, our hopes are answered.
You said the enemy would not come down
But keep the hills and upper regions.
It proves not so, their battles are at hand.
5 They mean to warn us at Philippi here,
Answering before we do demand of them.

Antony. Tut! I am in their bosoms and I know
Wherefore they do it. They could be content
To visit other places, and come down
10 With fearful bravery, thinking by this face
To fasten in our thoughts that they have courage.
But 'tis not so.

[Enter a Messenger.]

Messenger.　　　Prepare you, generals,
The enemy comes on in gallant show;
15 Their bloody sign of battle is hung out,
And something to be done immediately.

Antony. Octavius, lead your battle softly on

20 *exigent:* moment of crisis.

22 *They . . . parley:* They are standing and waiting for a conference.

25 *answer on their charge:* respond to their attack.

37-39 *The posture . . . honeyless:* We don't know yet how effective you'll be as a soldier, but your words are sweeter than honey. (Hybla is a mountain in Sicily known for its sweet honey.)

Upon the left hand of the even field.

Octavius. Upon the right hand I. Keep thou the left.

20   **Antony.** Why do you cross me in this exigent?

Octavius. I do not cross you; but I will do so.

[March.]

*[Drum. Enter Brutus, Cassius, and their Army; Lucilius,
Titinius, Messala, and others.]*

Brutus. They stand and would have parley.

Cassius. Stand fast, Titinius. We must out and talk.

Octavius. Mark Antony, shall we give sign of battle?

25   **Antony.** No, Caesar, we will answer on their charge.
        Make forth. The generals would have some words.

Octavius. Stir not until the signal.

*[Brutus, Cassius, Octavius, and Antony meet in the center
of the stage.]*

Brutus. Words before blows. Is it so, countrymen?

Octavius. Not that we love words better, as you do.

30   **Brutus.** Good words are better than bad strokes,
        Octavius.

Antony. In your bad strokes, Brutus, you give good
        words;
        Witness the hole you made in Caesar's heart,
35   Crying "Long live! Hail, Caesar!"

Cassius.   Antony,
        The posture of your blows are yet unknown;
        But for your words, they rob the Hybla bees,
        And leave them honeyless.

40   **Antony.**   Not stingless too.

Brutus. O yes, and soundless too!

44-50 *You did not so . . . neck:* You didn't give warning before you killed Caesar. Instead, you acted like loving pets and slaves while Casca, like a dog *(cur)*, stabbed Caesar in the neck.

51-53 *Now . . . ruled:* Cassius angrily tells Brutus that they wouldn't be listening to these insults if he had had his way *(Cassius might have ruled)* when arguing that Antony should be killed.

54-56 *Come . . . drops:* Get to the point *(cause)*. Arguing is tiresome. We will settle it by shedding blood.

61-62 *or till . . . traitors:* or until a second Caesar (that is, Octavius himself—Caesar's grandnephew and adopted son) has been killed by the traitors.

63-64 *Caesar . . . with thee:* Brutus here refers to Octavius, who took that name. The only way you'll die from a traitor's hands is if you kill yourself, Brutus insists.

70-71 *masker . . . still:* Cassius is insulting Antony by calling him a party-goer and a playboy. Same old Cassius *(Old Cassius still),* Antony replies.

For you have stol'n their buzzing, Antony,
And very wisely threat before you sting.

Antony. Villains! you did not so when your vile daggers
45   Hacked one another in the sides of Caesar.
You showed your teeth like apes, and fawned like
      hounds,
And bowed like bondmen, kissing Caesar's feet;
Whilst damned Casca, like a cur, behind
50   Struck Caesar on the neck. O you flatterers!

Cassius. Flatterers? Now, Brutus, thank yourself!
This tongue had not offended so today
If Cassius might have ruled.

Octavius. Come, come, the cause! If arguing make us
55   sweat,
The proof of it will turn to redder drops.
Look,
I draw a sword against conspirators.
When think you that the sword goes up again?
60   Never, till Caesar's three-and-thirty wounds
Be well avenged, or till another Caesar
Have added slaughter to the sword of traitors.

Brutus. Caesar, thou canst not die by traitors' hands
Unless thou bring'st them with thee.

65 **Octavius.**   So I hope.
I was not born to die on Brutus' sword.

Brutus. Oh, if thou wert the noblest of thy strain,
Young man, thou couldst not die more honorable.

Cassius. A peevish schoolboy, worthless of such honor,
70   Joined with a masker and a reveller!

Antony. Old Cassius still.

Octavius.   Come, Antony. Away!
Defiance, traitor, hurl we in your teeth.
If you dare fight today, come to the field;

75 stomachs: enough nerve. *Does the prebattle meeting seem believable? Has anything been accomplished?*

78 all . . . hazard: Everything is at stake.

86-88 against . . . liberties: I am forced to gamble the freedom of Rome on one battle. *What does he mean?*

89-101 I held . . . give up the ghost: Epicurus was a philosopher who did not believe omens. Cassius says that he once was a follower of this philosophy, but now he sometimes believes in things that predict the future **(credit things that do presage).** Cassius then tells Messala of two eagles that accompanied the army from Sardis to Philippi. The eagles have been replaced by ravens, crows, and hawks **(kites)**—birds that symbolize death.

92 former ensign: the flag that was carried at the head of the army's march.

75   If not, when you have stomachs.

[*Exeunt* Octavious, Antony, *and their Army.*]

Cassius. Why, now blow wind, swell billow, and swim
       bark!
    The storm is up, and all is on the hazard.

Brutus. Ho, Lucilius! Hark, a word with you.

[*Lucilius and* Messala *stand forth.*]

80 **Lucilius.**   My lord?

[*Brutus and* Lucilius *converse apart.*]

Cassius. Messala.

Messala.   What says my general?

Cassius.   Messala,
    This is my birthday; as this very day
85   Was Cassius born. Give me thy hand, Messala.
    Be thou my witness that against my will
    (As Pompey was) am I compelled to set
    Upon one battle all our liberties.
    You know that I held Epicurus strong
90   And his opinion. Now I change my mind
    And partly credit things that do presage.
    Coming from Sardis, on our former ensign
    Two mighty eagles fell, and there they perched,
    Gorging and feeding from our soldiers' hands,
95   Who to Philippi here consorted us.
    This morning are they fled away and gone,
    And in their steads do ravens, crows, and kites
    Fly o'er our heads and downward look on us
    As we were sickly prey. Their shadows seem
100   A canopy most fatal, under which
    Our army lies, ready to give up the ghost.

Messala. Believe not so.

Cassius.   I but believe it partly,

105 *constantly:* with determination.

111 *Let's . . . befall:* Let's think about the worst that might happen to us.

115-122 *Even . . . govern us below:* Brutus reminds Cassius that Brutus' philosophy (Stoicism) says people should endure their troubles. Therefore, Brutus should not believe in suicide. He mentions Cato, a famous Roman who killed himself after Pompey lost to Caesar.

131 *our . . . take:* Let's make a final farewell to each other.

For I am fresh of spirit and resolved
105 To meet all perils very constantly.

Brutus. Even so, Lucilius.

Cassius.   Now, most noble Brutus,
The gods today stand friendly, that we may,
Lovers in peace, lead on our days to age!
110 But since the affairs of men rest still incertain,
Let's reason with the worst that may befall.
If we do lose this battle, then is this
The very last time we shall speak together.
What are you then determined to do?

115 **Brutus.** Even by the rule of that philosophy
By which I did blame Cato for the death
Which he did give himself—I know not how,
But I do find it cowardly and vile,
For fear of what might fall, so to prevent
120 The time of life—arming myself with patience
To stay the providence of some high powers
That govern us below.

Cassius.   Then, if we lose this battle,
You are contented to be led in triumph
125 Through the streets of Rome.

Brutus. No, Cassius, no. Think not, thou noble Roman,
That ever Brutus will go bound to Rome.
He bears too great a mind. But this same day
Must end that work the ides of March begun,
130 And whether we shall meet again I know not.
Therefore our everlasting farewell take.
For ever and for ever farewell, Cassius!
If we do meet again, why, we shall smile;
If not, why then this parting was well made.

135 **Cassius.** For ever and for ever farewell, Brutus!
If we do meet again, we'll smile indeed;
If not, 'tis true this parting was well made.

1-2 *give . . . side:* Give these orders to our soldiers on that side of the field.

4 *cold demeanor:* lack of courage. *How does Brutus feel about the battle at this point?*

Brutus. Why then, lead on. O that a man might know
The end of this day's business ere it come!
140 But it sufficeth that the day will end,
And then the end is known. Come, ho! Away!

[Exeunt]

Scene 2 *The battlefield.*

*Brutus sends Messala with orders for the
forces across the field.*

[Alarum. Enter Brutus and Messala.]

Brutus. Ride, ride, Messala, ride, and give these bills
Unto the legions on the other side.

[Loud alarum.]

Let them set on at once; for I perceive
But cold demeanor in Octavius' wing,
5 And sudden push gives them the overthrow.
Ride, ride, Messala! Let them all come down.

[Exeunt.]

Scene 3 *Another part of the battlefield.*

*Cassius retreats, losing the battle to Antony's
forces. He sends Titinius to see if nearby forces
are friend or enemy. From a hill, Pindarus
believes he sees Titinius killed. Completely
discouraged, Cassius asks Pindarus to kill him.
Titinius returns to find Cassius' body and kills
himself. Brutus and others arrive, having
defeated Octavius's army. Messala has brought
them to see the body of Cassius. Now they see
that Titinius is also dead. Brutus mourns the
two, but also looks to a second battle with his
enemies.*

[Enter Cassius and Titinius.]

1-4 ***The villains . . . him:*** Cassius is watching his men run
away ***(fly)*** from the battle. He killed his own flag-
bearer (the dead ***ensign*** lying on the ground near him)
when he saw the man running away. *How does
Cassius seem to feel about the battle?*

7 ***His . . . spoil:*** Brutus' soldiers began looting (instead
of fighting the enemy).

16-19 ***Mount . . . enemy:*** Ride my horse to those troops
over there, and come back to tell me if they are friend
or enemy.

20 ***even with a thought:*** as fast as you can think of it.

26 ***is run his compass:*** has come full circle (that is, my
life is complete). *What is Cassius planning to do?*

Cassius. O, look, Titinius, look! The villains fly!
  Myself have to mine own turned enemy.
  This ensign here of mine was turning back;
  I slew the coward and did take it from him.

5 **Titinius.** O Cassius, Brutus gave the word too early,
  Who, having some advantage on Octavius,
  Took it too eagerly. His soldiers fell to spoil,
  Whilst we by Antony are all enclosed.

[Enter Pindarus.]

Pindarus. Fly further off, my lord! fly further off!
10   Mark Antony is in your tents, my lord.
  Fly, therefore, noble Cassius, fly far off!

Cassius. This hill is far enough. Look, look, Titinius!
  Are those my tents where I perceive the fire?

Titinius. They are, my lord.

15 **Cassius.**   Titinius, if thou lovest me,
  Mount thou my horse and hide thy spurs in him
  Till he have brought thee up to yonder troops
  And here again, that I may rest assured
  Whether yond troops are friend or enemy.

20 **Titinius.** I will be here again even with a thought.

[Exit.]

Cassius. Go, Pindarus, get higher on that hill.
  My sight was ever thick. Regard Titinius,
  And tell me what thou not'st about the field.

[Pindarus ascends the hill.]

  This day I breathed first. Time is come round,
25   And where I did begin, there shall I end.
  My life is run his compass. Sirrah, what news?

Pindarus.

[Above.]

31-37 From a distance, Pindarus describes the capture of Titinuis.

40 *ta'en:* taken (captured).

42-50 *In Parthia . . . the sword:* When I saved your life in Parthia (an ancient Asian land), you swore to do whatever I asked. Now keep your oath and become a free man. I'll cover my face as you stab me *(search this bosom)* with the same knife that killed Caesar. Don't argue *(Stand not to answer).* Why does Cassius finally decide to kill himself?

53-54 *So . . . will:* I am free; but I wouldn't have been if I had done what I wanted (that is, refused to kill Cassius).

O my lord!

Cassius. What news?

30 **Pindarus.**

[Above.]

    Titinius is enclosed round about
    With horsemen that make to him on the spur.
    Yet he spurs on. Now they are almost on him.
    Now, Titinius!
35   Now some light. O, he lights too! He's ta'en.

[Shout.]

    And hark!
    They shout for joy.

Cassius.   Come down; behold no more.
    O coward that I am to live so long
40   To see my best friend ta'en before my face!

[Enter Pindarus *from above.]*

    Come hither, sirrah.
    In Parthia did I take thee prisoner,
    And then I swore thee, saving of thy life,
    That whatsoever I did bid thee do,
45   Thou shouldst attempt it. Come now, keep thine oath.
    Now be a freeman, and with this good sword,
    That ran through Caesar's bowels, search this bosom.
    Stand not to answer. Here, take thou the hilts,
    And when my face is covered, as 'tis now,
50   Guide thou the sword.

*[*Pindarus *stabs him.]*

    —Caesar, thou are revenged
    Even with the sword that killed thee.

[Dies.]

Pindarus. So, I am free, yet would not so have been,
    Durst I have done my will. O Cassius!

57-59 *It is . . . Antony:* It's an even exchange. Just as Antony has defeated Cassius, Brutus has defeated Octavius.

62 *disconsolate:* extremely sad.

75-79 *O hateful . . . thee:* Why do mistaken beliefs, which come from sadness *(Melancholy's child),* always seem so true when they are false? A mistake is easily born but always kills its mother at birth.

84 *darts envenomed:* poisoned darts.

Far from this country Pindarus shall run,
Where never Roman shall take note of him.

[Exit.]

[Reenter Titinius with Messala.]

Messala. It is but change, Titinius; for Octavius
Is overthrown by noble Brutus' power,
As Cassius' legions are by Antony.

60 **Titinius.** These tidings will well comfort Cassius.

Messala. Where did you leave him?

Titinius.   All disconsolate,
With Pindarus his bondman, on this hill.

65 **Titinius.** He lies not like the living. O my heart!

Messala. Is not that he?

Titinius.   No, this was he, Messala,
But Cassius is no more. O setting sun,
As in thy red rays thou does sink to night
70 So in his red blood Cassius' day is set!
The sun of Rome is set. Our day is gone;
Clouds, dews, and dangers come; our deeds are done!
Mistrust of my success hath done this deed.

Messala. Mistrust of good success hath done this deed.
75 O hateful Error, Melancholy's child,
Why dost thou show to the apt thoughts of men
The things that are not? O Error, soon conceived,
Thou never com'st unto a happy birth,
But kill'st the mother that engend'red thee!

80 **Titinius.** What, Pindarus! Where art thou, Pindarus?

Messala. Seek him, Titinius, whilst I go to meet
The noble Brutus, thrusting this report
Into his ears. I may say "thrusting" it;
For piercing steel and darts envenomed
85 Shall be as welcome to the ears of Brutus

87 *Hie you:* Hurry.

94 *misconstrued:* misunderstood. *What was the mistake that led to Cassius' suicide?*

95 Titinius removes the laurel wreath his friends put on his head to symbolize his victory. In his grief, he puts the wreath on Cassius' head.

97 *apace:* quickly.

99 *This . . . part:* This (killing myself) is the proper thing for a brave Roman to do. *Why does Titinius believe this is the right thing to do?*

109 *whe'r:* whether.

110-113 *Are yet . . . fellow:* Are there two Romans still living who are as good as these two? I bid you both farewell. Rome will never see your equal *(breed thy fellow).*

As tidings of this sight.

Titinius.   Hie you, Messala,
And I will seek for Pindarus the while.

[Exit Messala.]

[Titinius looks at Cassius.]

Why didst thou send me forth, brave Cassius?
90   Did I not meet thy friends, and did not they
Put on my brows this wreath of victory
And bid me give it thee? Didst thou not hear their
shouts?
Alas, thou hast misconstrued everything!
95   But hold thee, take this garland on thy brow.
Thy Brutus bid me give it thee, and I
Will do his bidding. Brutus, come apace
And see how I regarded Caius Cassius.
By your leave, gods. This is a Roman's part.
100   Come, Cassius' sword, and find Titinius' heart.

[Dies.]

*[Alarum. Enter Brutus, Messala, young Cato, Strato,
Volumnius, and Lucilius.]*

Brutus. Where, where, Messala, doth his body lie?

Messala. Lo, yonder, and Titinius mourning it.

Brutus. Titinius' face is upward.

Cato.   He is slain.

105 **Brutus.** O Julius Caesar, thou art mighty yet!
Thy spirit walks abroad and turns our swords
In our own proper entrails.

[Low alarums.]

Cato.   Brave Titinius!
Look whe'r he have not crowned dead Cassius.

110 **Brutus.** Are yet two Romans living such as these?

116 *Thasos* **(thā′ säs′):** an island near Philippi.

122 *We shall . . . fight:* We'll try our luck in a second battle.

4 *Marcus Cato:* Portia's father, a greatly respected Roman.

The last of all the Romans, fare thee well!
It is impossible that ever Rome
Should breed thy fellow. Friends, I owe more tears
To this dead man than you shall see me pay.
115 I shall find time, Cassius; I shall find time.
Come therefore, and to Thasos send his body.
His funerals shall not be in our camp,
Lest it discomfort us. Lucilius, come;
And come, young Cato. Let us to the field.
120 Labeo and Flavius set our battles on.
'Tis three o'clock; and, Romans, yet ere night
We shall try fortune in a second fight.

[Exeunt.]

Scene 4 *Another part of the field.*

*During the battle, young Cato is killed and
Lucilius taken prisoner. Brought to Antony,
Lucilius insists that Brutus will never be taken
alive.*

[Alarum. *Enter* Brutus, Messala, Young Cato, Lucilius, *and*
Flavius.]

Brutus. Yet, countrymen, O, yet hold up your heads!

Cato. What fellow doth not? Who will go with me?
I will proclaim my name about the field.
I am the son of Marcus Cato, ho!
5   A foe to tyrants, and my country's friend.
I am the son of Marcus Cato, ho!

[Enter Soldiers *and fight.*]

Brutus. And I am Brutus, Marcus Brutus I!
Brutus, my country's friend! Know me for Brutus!

[Exit.]

[Young Cato *falls.*]

12 *Yield:* surrender.

14-15 *There is . . . death:* This money is for you, if you will kill me immediately *(straight).* If you kill Brutus, you will win honor for it. Lucilius pretends to be Brutus and fools the soldier.

21-23 *Do you agree with Lucilius that Brutus will never be taken alive?*

27-29 *Why do you think Antony is being so merciful to Lucilius?*

Lucilius. O young and noble Cato, art thou down?
10   Why, now thou diest as bravely as Titinius,
      And mayst be honored, being Cato's son.

First Soldier. Yield, or thou diest.

Lucilius.   Only I yield to die.

[Offering money.]

      There is so much that thou wilt kill me straight.
15   Kill Brutus, and be honored in his death.

First Soldier. We must not. A noble prisoner!

[Enter Antony.]

Second Soldier. Room ho! Tell Antony Brutus is ta'en.

First Soldier. I'll tell the news. Here comes the general.
      Brutus is ta'en! Brutus, is ta'en, my lord!

20 **Antony.** Where is he?

Lucilius. Safe, Antony; Brutus is safe enough.
      I dare assure thee that no enemy
      Shall ever take alive the noble Brutus.
      The gods defend him from so great a shame!
25   When you do find him, or alive or dead,
      He will be found like Brutus, like himself.

Antony. This is not Brutus, friend; but, I assure you,
      A prize no less in worth. Keep this man safe;
      Give him all kindness. I had rather have
30   Such men my friends than enemies. Go on,
      And see whe'r Brutus be alive or dead;
      And bring us word unto Octavius' tent
      How everything is chanced.

[Exeunt.]

2-3 ***Statilius . . . slain:*** Statilius (our scout) signaled with his torch that all was well at our camp. But since he hasn't come back, he has been either captured or killed.

4-10 Brutus says that it has become fashionable to kill, not to capture. Then he whispers something to Clitus, who seems shocked by what Brutus has asked him to do. Brutus whispers the same request to Dardanius, who reacts the same way. After this, Brutus walks away from the two men.

17 ***List:*** listen to.

Scene 5 *Another part of the battlefield.*

Facing defeat, Brutus' forces rest. Brutus feels that all is lost. He asks three men to kill him, but each refuses. Finally, Strato agrees to hold the sword as Brutus kills himself on it. Antony, Octavius, and others arrive. Antony mourns Brutus, calling him the "noblest Roman." Octavius promises him a noble funeral as the play ends.

[Enter Brutus, Dardanius, Clitus, Strato, and Volumnius.]

Brutus. Come, poor remains of friends, rest on this rock.

Clitus. Statilius showed the torchlight but, my lord,
He came not back. He is or ta'en or slain.

Brutus. Sit thee down, Clitus. Slaying is the word.
5   It is a deed in fashion. Hark thee, Clitus.

[Whispers.]

Clitus. What, I, my lord? No, not for all the world!

Brutus. Peace then. No words.

Clitus.   I'll rather kill myself.

Brutus. Hark thee, Dardanius.

[Whispers.]

10 **Dardanius.**   Shall I do such a deed?

Clitus. O Dardanius!

Dardanius. O Clitus!

Clitus. What ill request did Brutus make to thee?

Dardanius. To kill him, Clitus. Look he meditates.

15 **Clitus.** Now is that noble vessel full of grief,
That it runs over even at his eyes.

Brutus. Come hither, good Volumnius. List a word.

Volumnius. What says my lord?

21 *Two several times:* twice.

27 *pit:* a hole into which hunted animals are forced. *How does Brutus seem to feel about the battle now?*

29 *tarry:* wait.

31-32 *I prithee . . . on it:* I beg you to hold my sword (on the ground, with the blade pointing up) while I fall onto it.

33 *That's . . . friend:* That's no duty for a friend to perform.

38-39 Think about how Brutus sums up his life in these two lines. Then think about the way Cassius manipulated him in Act One, and the way Antony fooled him into letting Antony speak to the crowd. *What can you conclude about Brutus' understanding of people?*

45-46 *my bones . . . hour:* My tired bones have worked to bring me to this final hour of rest.

Brutus.   Why this, Volumnius.

20   The ghost of Caesar hath appeared to me
Two several times by night—at Sardis once,
And this last night here in Philippi fields.
I know my hour is come.

Volumnius.   Not so, my lord.

25 **Brutus.** Nay, I am sure it is, Volumnius.
Thou seest the world, Volumnius, how it goes.
Our enemies have beat us to the pit.

[Low alarums.]

It is more worthy to leap in ourselves
Than tarry till they push us. Good Volumnius,
30   Thou know'st that we two went to school together.
Even for that our love of old, I prithee
Hold thou my sword-hilts whilst I run on it.

Volumnius. That's not an office for a friend, my lord.

[Alarum still.]

Clitus. Fly, fly, my lord! There is no tarrying here.

35 **Brutus.** Farewell to you; and you; and you, Volumnius.
Strato, thou hast been all this while asleep.
Farewell to thee too, Strato. Countrymen,
My heart doth joy that yet in all my life
I found no man but he was true to me.
40   I shall have glory by this losing day
More than Octavius and Mark Antony
By this vile conquest shall attain unto.
So fare you well at once, for Brutus' tongue
Hath almost ended his life's history.
45   Night hangs upon mine eyes; my bones would rest,
That have but labored to attain this hour.

[Alarum. Cry within:]

                              Fly, fly, fly!

52 *smatch:* little bit.

57 *I killed . . . will:* I didn't kill you (Caesar) half as
willingly as I kill myself.

59 *man:* servant.

64-66 *So Brutus . . . true:* That is just how Brutus should be
found. Thank you, Brutus, for proving me correct (in
saying you would never be taken alive).

67-68 *All . . . me:* All those who served Brutus will now be
welcome in my army. Strato *(Fellow),* will you join me?

69 *prefer:* recommend.

Clitus. Fly, my lord, fly!

Brutus.   Hence! I will follow.

[Exeunt Clitus, Dardanius, and Volumnius.]

50   I prithee, Strato, stay thou by thy lord.
     Thou art a fellow of a good respect;
     Thy life hath had some smatch of honor in it.
     Hold then my sword, and turn away thy face
     While I do run upon it. Wilt thou, Strato?

55   **Strato.** Give me your hand first. Fare you well, my lord.

Brutus. Farewell, good Strato. Caesar, now be still.
     I killed not thee with half so good a will.

[Dies.]

[Alarum. Retreat. Enter Octavius, Antony, Messala, Lucilius, and the Army.]

Octavius. What man is that?

Messala. My master's man. Strato, where is thy master?

60   **Strato.** Free from the bondage you are in, Messala.
     The conquerors can but make a fire of him;
     For Brutus only overcame himself,
     And no man else hath honor by his death.

Lucilius. So Brutus should be found. I thank thee,
65   Brutus,
     That thou hast proved Lucilius' saying true.

Octavius. All that served Brutus, I will entertain them.
     Fellow, wilt thou bestow thy time with me?

Strato. Ay, if Messala will prefer me to you.

70   **Octavius.** Do so, good Messala.

Messala. How died my master, Strato?

Strato. I held the sword, and he did run on it.

73-74 *Octavius . . . master:* Octavius, I recommend him for your army; he performed the last favor for Brutus *(my master).*

75-82 Now that the war is won, Antony pays a final tribute to Brutus. *What good qualities of Brutus does Antony mention in this tribute?*

76 *save:* except.

79 *made one of them:* joined the conspirators.

83 *According . . . him:* Let us treat him as he deserves.

88 *part:* divide up.

Messala. Octavius, then take him to follow thee,
That did the latest service to my master.

75 **Antony.** This was the noblest Roman of them all.
All the conspirators save only he
Did that they did in envy of great Caesar;
He, only in a general honest thought
And common good to all, made one of them.
80 His life was gentle, and the elements
So mixed in him that Nature might stand up
And say to all the world, "This was a man!"

Octavius. According to his virtue let us use him,
With all respect and rites of burial.
85 Within my tent his bones tonight shall lie,
Most like a soldier, ordered honorably.
So call the field to rest, and let's away
To part the glories of this happy day.

[Exeunt.]

RELATED READINGS

The Life of Caesar

by Suetonius
translated by Robert Graves

*Shakespeare's Julius Caesar " . . . doth
bestride the narrow world like a Colossus."
How mighty was the real Julius Caesar?
Over a century after Caesar's death in 44
B.C., Suetonius, a Roman historian, wrote a
compelling biography of this powerful
leader.*

Caesar is said to have been tall, fair, and well-built, with a rather broad face and keen, dark-brown eyes. His health was sound, apart from sudden comas and a tendency to nightmares which troubled him towards the end of his life; but he twice had epileptic fits while on campaign. He was something of a dandy, always keeping his head carefully trimmed and shaved. . . . His baldness was a disfigurement which his enemies harped upon, much to his exasperation; but he used to comb the thin strands of hair forward from his poll, and of all the honours voted him by the Senate and People, none pleased him so much as the privilege of wearing a laurel wreath on all occasions—he constantly took advantage of it. . . .

His affairs with women are commonly described as numerous and extravagant: among those of noble birth whom he is said to have seduced were Servius Sulpicius' wife Postumia; Aulus Gabinius' wife Lollia; Marcus Crassus' wife Tertulla; and even Pompey's wife Mucia. . . .

Among his mistresses were several queens— including Eunoë, wife of Bogudes the Moor whom, according to Marcus Actorius Naso, he loaded with presents; Bogudes is said to have profited equally. The most famous of these queens was Cleopatra of Egypt. He often feasted with her until dawn; and they would have sailed together in her state barge nearly to Ethiopia had his soldiers consented to follow him. He eventually summoned Cleopatra to Rome, and would not let her return to Alexandria without high titles and rich presents. He even allowed her to call the son whom she had borne him by his own name. . . .

Yet not even his enemies denied that he drank abstemiously. An epigram of Marcus Cato's survives: 'Caesar was the only sober man who ever tried to wreck the Constitution'; and Gaius Oppius relates that he cared so little for good food that when once he attended a dinner party where rancid oil had been served by mistake, and all the other guests refused it, Caesar helped himself more liberally than usual, to show that he did not consider his host either careless or boorish.

He was not particularly honest in money matters, either while a provincial governor or while holding office at Rome. Several memoirs record that as Governor in Spain he not only begged his allies for money to settle his debts, but wantonly sacked several Lusitanian towns, though they had accepted his terms and opened their gates to welcome him. . . .

Caesar was a most skilful swordsman and horseman, and showed surprising powers of endurance. He always led his army, more often on foot than in the saddle, went bareheaded in sun and rain alike, and could travel for long distances at incredible speed in a gig, taking very little luggage. If he reached an unfordable river he would either swim or propel himself across it on an inflated skin; and often arrived at his destination before the messengers whom he had sent ahead to announce his approach. . . .

Sometimes he fought after careful tactical planning, sometimes on the spur of the moment—at the end of a march, often; or in miserable weather, when he would be least expected to make a move. Towards the end of his life, however, he took fewer chances; having come to the conclusion that his unbroken run of victories ought to sober him, now that he could not possibly gain more by winning yet another battle than he would lose by a defeat. It was his rule never to let enemy troops rally when he had routed them, and always therefore to assault their camp at once. If the fight were a hard-fought one he used to send the chargers away—his own among the first—as a warning that those who feared to stand their ground need not hope to escape on horseback. . . .

If Caesar's troops gave ground he would often rally them in person, catching individual fugitives by the throat and forcing them round to face the enemy again; even if they were panic-stricken—as when one standard-bearer threatened him with the sharp butt of his Eagle and another, whom he tried to detain, ran off leaving the Eagle in his hand.

Caesar's reputation for determination is fully borne out by the instances quoted. After Pharsalus, he had sent his legions ahead of him into Asia and was crossing the Hellespont in a small ferry-boat, when Lucius Cassius with ten naval vessels approached. Caesar made no attempt to escape but rowed towards the flagship and demanded Cassius' surrender; Cassius gave it and stepped aboard Caesar's craft.

Again, while attacking a bridge at Alexandria, Caesar was forced by a sudden enemy sortie to jump into a row-boat. So many of his men followed him that he dived into the sea and swam 200 yards until he reached the nearest Caesarean ship—holding his left hand above water the whole way to keep certain documents dry; and towing his purple cloak behind him with his teeth, to save this trophy from the Egyptians.

He judged his men by their fighting record, not by their morals or social position, treating them all with equal severity—and equal indulgence; since it was only in the presence of the enemy that he insisted on strict discipline. He never gave forewarning of a march or a battle, but kept his troops always on the alert for sudden orders to go wherever he directed. Often he made them turn out when there was no need at all, especially in wet weather or on public holidays. Sometimes he would say: 'Keep a close eye on me!' and then steal away from camp at any hour of the day or night, expecting them to follow. It was certain to be a particularly long march, and hard on stragglers. . . .

Nobody can deny that during the Civil War, and after, he behaved with wonderful restraint and clemency. Whereas Pompey declared that all who were not actively with the government were against it and would be treated as public enemies, Caesar announced that all who were not actively against him were with him. He allowed every centurion whom he had appointed on Pompey's recommendation to join the Pompeian forces if he pleased. . . .

During the battle of Pharsalus he shouted to his men: 'Spare your fellow-Romans!' and then allowed them to save one enemy soldier apiece, whoever he might be. . . .

Yet other deeds and sayings of Caesar's may be set to the debit account, and justify the conclusion that he deserved assassination. Not only did he accept excessive honours, such as a life-consulship, a life-dictatorship, a perpetual Censorship, the title 'Imperator' put before his name, and the title 'Father of his Country' appended to it, also a statue standing among those of the ancient kings, and a raised couch placed in the orchestra at the Theatre; but took other honours which, as a mere mortal, he should certainly have refused. These included a golden throne in the Senate House, and another on the tribunal; a ceremonial chariot and litter for carrying his statue in the religious procession around the Circus; temples, altars, and divine images; a priest of his own cult; a new college of Lupercals to celebrate his divinity; and the renaming of the seventh month as 'July'. Few, in fact, were the honours which he was not pleased to accept or assume.

His third and fourth consulships were merely titular; the dictatorship conferred on him at the same time supplied all the authority he needed. And in both years he substituted two new Consuls for himself during the last quarter, meanwhile letting only tribunes and aediles of the people be elected, and appointing prefects instead of praetors to govern the city during his absence.

One of the Consuls died suddenly on New Year's Eve and, when someone asked to hold office for the remaining few hours, Caesar granted his request. He showed equal scorn of traditional precedent by choosing magistrates several years ahead, decorating ten former praetors with the emblems of consular rank, and admitting to the Senate men of foreign birth, including semi-civilized Gauls, who had been granted Roman citizenship. He placed his own slaves in charge of the Mint and the public revenues, and sent one of his favourites, a freedman's son, to command the three legions stationed at Alexandria.

Titus Ampius has recorded some of Caesar's public statements which reveal a similar presumption: that the Republic was nothing—a mere name without form or substance; that Sulla had proved himself a dunce by resigning his dictatorship; and that, now his own word was law, people ought to be more careful how they approached him. Once, when a soothsayer reported that a sacrificial beast had been found to have no heart—an unlucky omen indeed—Caesar told him arrogantly: 'The omens will be more favourable when I wish them to be; meanwhile I am not at all surprised that a beast should lack the organ which inspires our finer feelings.'

What made the Romans hate him so bitterly was that when, one day, the entire Senate, armed with an imposing list of honours that they had just voted him, came to where he sat in front of the Temple of Mother Venus, he did not rise to greet them. According to some accounts he would have risen had not Cornelius Balbus prevented him; according to others, he made no such move and grimaced angrily at Gaius Trebatius who suggested this courtesy. The case was aggravated by a memory of Caesar's behaviour during one of his triumphs: he had ridden past the benches reserved for the tribunes of the people, and shouted in fury at a certain Pontius Aquila, who had kept his seat: 'Hey, there, Aquila the tribune! Do you want me to restore the Republic?' For several days after this incident he added to every undertaking he gave: 'With the kind consent of Pontius Aquila.'

This open insult to the Senate was emphasized by an even worse example of his arrogance. As he returned to Rome from the Alban Hill, where the Latin Festival had been celebrated, a member of the crowd set a laurel wreath bound with a royal white fillet on the head of his statue. Two tribunes of the people, Epidius Marullus and Caesetius Flavus, ordered the fillet to be removed at once and the offender imprisoned. But Caesar reprimanded and summarily deposed them both: either because the suggestion that he should be crowned King had been so rudely rejected, or else because—this was his own version—they had given him no chance to reject it himself and so earn deserved credit. From that day forward, however, he lay under the odious suspicion of having tried to revive the title of King; though, indeed, when the commons greeted him with 'Long live the King!' he now protested: 'No,

I am Caesar, not King'; and though, again, when he was addressing the crowd from the Rostra at the Lupercalian Festival, and Mark Antony, the Consul, made several attempts to crown him, he refused the offer each time and at last sent the crown away for dedication to Capitoline Jupiter. What made matters worse was a persistent rumour that Caesar intended to move the seat of government to Troy or Alexandria, carrying off all the national resources, drafting every available man in Italy for military service, and letting his friends govern the city. At the next meeting of the House (it was further whispered), Lucius Cotta would announce a decision of the Fifteen who had charge of the Sibylline Books, that since these prophetic writings stated clearly: 'Only a king can conquer the Parthians,' the title of King must be conferred on Caesar. . . .

More than sixty conspirators banded together against him, led by Gaius Cassius and Marcus and Decimus Brutus. A suggested plan was to wait until the consular elections, when Caesar would take his stand on the wooden bridge along which voters walked to the poll; one group of conspirators would then topple him over, while another waited underneath with daggers drawn. An alternative was to attack him in the Sacred Way or at the entrance to the Theatre. The conspirators wavered between these plans until Caesar called a meeting of the Senate in the Pompeian Assembly Room for the Ides of March; they then decided at once that this would be a convenient time and place.

Unmistakable signs forewarned Caesar of his assassination. . . . During a sacrifice, the augur Spurinna warned Caesar that the danger threatening him would not come later than the Ides of March.

These warnings, and ill-health, made him hesitate for some time whether to go ahead with his plans, or whether to postpone the meeting. Finally Decimus Brutus persuaded him not to disappoint the Senate, who had been in full session for some time, waiting for him to arrive. It was about ten o'clock when he set off for the House. As he went, someone handed him a note containing details of the plot against his life, but he merely added it to the bundle of petitions in his left hand, which he intended to read later. Several victims were then sacrificed, and despite consistently unfavourable omens, he entered the House, deriding Spurinna as a false prophet. 'The Ides of March have come,' he said. 'Yes, they have come,' replied Spurinna, 'but they have not yet gone.'

As soon as Caesar took his seat the conspirators crowded around him as if to pay their respects. Tillius Cimber, who had taken the lead, came up close, pretending to ask a question. Caesar made a gesture of postponement, but Cimber caught hold of his shoulders. 'This is violence!' Caesar cried, and at that moment, as he turned away, one of the Casca brothers with a sweep of his dagger stabbed him just below the throat. Caesar grasped Casca's arm and ran it through with his stylus; he was leaping away when another dagger blow stopped him. Confronted by a ring of drawn daggers, he drew the top of his gown over his face, and at the same time ungirded the lower part, letting it fall to his feet so that he would die with both legs decently covered. Twenty-three dagger thrusts went home as he stood there. Caesar did not utter a sound after Casca's blow had drawn a groan from him; though some say that when he saw Marcus Brutus about to deliver the second blow, he reproached him in Greek with: 'You, too, my child?'

The entire Senate then dispersed in confusion, and Caesar was left lying dead for some time until three slave boys carried him home in a litter, with one arm hanging over the side.

Epitaph on a Tyrant

by W. H. Auden

*Do Caesar's ambition, success, and
popularity spell the end of the Roman
Republic and its tradition of democratic
government? Alarmed that Caesar will
abuse his power, Cassius, Brutus, and the
other conspirators plot to assassinate him,
though he has not yet actually committed
any acts of tyranny. Why fear a tyrant?*

Perfection, of a kind, was what he was after,
And the poetry he invented was easy to
    understand;
He knew human folly like the back of his
    hand,
And was greatly interested in armies and
    fleets;
5 When he laughed, respectable senators burst
    with laughter,
And when he cried the little children died in
    the streets.

News Flash: Political Assassinations

After the conspirators have assassinated Caesar, Cassius declares, "How many ages hence/Shall this our lofty scene be acted over/In states unborn and accents yet unknown!" (Act Three, Scene 1, lines 122–124). Cassius understood that history repeats itself.

Lincoln Assassinated!

by a staff correspondent
(*New York Herald,* April 15, 1865)

IMPORTANT.

ASSASSINATION
OF
PRESIDENT LINCOLN.

The President Shot at the
Theatre Last Evening.

SECRETARY SEWARD
DAGGERED IN HIS BED,
BUT
NOT MORTALLY WOUNDED.

Clarence and Frederick Seward Badly Hurt.

ESCAPE OF THE ASSASSINS.

Intense Excitement in
Washington.

Scene at the Deathbed of
Mr. Lincoln.

First Dispatch

Washington, April 14, 1865.
Assassination has been inaugurated in Washington.
The bowie knife and pistol have been applied to
President Lincoln and Secretary Seward. The former
was shot in the throat, while at Ford's theatre tonight. Mr. Seward was badly cut about the neck, while
in his bed at his residence.

Second Dispatch

Washington, April 14, 1865.
An attempt was made about ten o'clock this evening
to assassinate the President and Secretary Seward. The
President was shot at Ford's Theatre. Result not yet
known. Mr. Seward's throat was cut, and his son
badly wounded.

There is intense excitement here.

DETAILS OF THE ASSASSINATION

Washington, April 14, 1865.

Washington was thrown into an intense excitement a few minutes before eleven o'clock this evening, by the announcement that the President and Secretary Seward had been assassinated and were dead.

The wildest excitement prevailed in all parts of the city. Men, women and children, old and young, rushed to and fro, and the rumors were magnified until we had nearly every member of the Cabinet killed. Some time elapsed before authentic data could be ascertained in regard to the affair.

The President and Mrs. Lincoln were at Ford's theatre, listening to the performance of *The American Cousin,* occupying a box in the second tier. At the close of the third act a person entered the box occupied by the President, and shot Mr. Lincoln in the head. The shot entered the back of his head, and came out above the temple.

The assassin then jumped from the box upon the stage and ran across to the other side, exhibiting a dagger in his hand, flourishing it in a tragical manner, shouting the same words repeated by the desperado at Mr. Seward's house, adding to it, "The South is avenged," and then escaped from the back entrance to the stage, but in his passage dropped his pistol and his hat.

Mr. Lincoln fell forward from his seat, and Mrs. Lincoln fainted.

The moment the astonished audience could realize what had happened, the President was taken and carried to Mr. Peterson's house, in Tenth Street, opposite to the theatre. Medical aid was immediately sent for, and the wound was at first supposed to be fatal, and it was announced that he could not live, but at half-past twelve he is still alive, though in a precarious condition.

As the assassin ran across the stage, Colonel J. B. Stewart, of this city, who was occupying one of the front seats in the orchestra, on the same side of the house as the box occupied by Mr. Lincoln, sprang to the stage and followed him; but he was obstructed in his passage across the stage by the fright of the actors, and reached the back door about three seconds after the assassin had passed out. Colonel Stewart got to the street just in time to see him mount his horse and ride away.

The operation shows that the whole thing was a preconcerted plan. The person who fired the pistol was a man about thirty years of age, about five feet nine, spare built, fair skin, dark hair, apparently bushy, with a large moustache. Laura Keene and the leader of the orchestra declare that they recognized him as J. Wilkes Booth the actor, and a rabid secessionist. Whoever he was, it is plainly evident that he thoroughly understood the theatre and all the approaches and modes of escape to the stage. A person not familiar with the theatre could not have possibly made his escape so well and quickly.

The alarm was sounded in every quarter. Mr. Stanton was notified, and immediately left his house.

All the other members of the Cabinet escaped attack.

Cavalrymen were sent out in all directions, and dispatches sent out to all the fortifications, and it is thought they will be captured.

About half-past ten o'clock this evening a tall, well dressed man made his appearance at Secretary Seward's residence, and applied for admission. He was refused admission by the servant, when the desperado stated that he had a prescription from the Surgeon General, and that he was ordered to deliver it in person. He was still refused, except upon the written order of the physician. This he pretended to show, and pushed by the servant and rushed up stairs to Mr. Seward's room. He was met at the door by Mr. Fred Seward, who notified him that he was master of the house, and would take charge of the medicine. After a few words had passed between them he dodged by Fred Seward and rushed to the Secretary's bed and struck him in the neck with a dagger, and also in the breast.

It was supposed at first that Mr. Seward was killed instantly, but it was found afterwards that the wound was not mortal.

Major Wm. H. Seward, Jr., paymaster, was in the room, and rushed to the defense of his father, and was badly cut in the *melee* with the assassin, but not fatally.

The desperado managed to escape from the house, and was prepared for escape by having a horse at the door. He immediately mounted his horse, and sung out the motto of the State of Virginia, *"Sic Semper Tyrannis!"* and rode off.

Surgeon General Barnes was immediately sent for, and he examined Mr. Seward and pronounced him safe. His wounds were not fatal. The jugular vein was not cut, nor the wound in the breast deep enough to be fatal.

Washington, April 15—1 A.M.

The streets in the vicinity of Ford's Theatre are densely crowded by an anxious and excited crowd. A guard has been placed across Tenth Street and F and K Streets, and only official persons and particular friends of the President are allowed to pass.

The popular heart is deeply stirred, and the deepest indignation against leading rebels is freely expressed.

The scene at the house where the President lies in *extremis* is very affecting. Even Secretary Stanton is affected to tears.

When the news spread through the city that the President had been shot, the people, with pale faces and compressed lips, crowded every place where there was the slightest chance of obtaining information in regard to the affair.

After the President was shot, Lieutenant Rathbun, caught the assassin by the arm, who immediately struck him with a knife, and jumped from the box, as before stated.

The popular affection for Mr. Lincoln has been shown by this diabolical assassination, which will bring eternal infamy, not only upon its authors, but upon the hellish cause which they desire to avenge.

Vice President Johnson arrived at the White House, where the President lies, about one o'clock, and will remain with him to the last.

The President's family are in attendance upon him also.

As soon as intelligence could be got to the War Department, the electric telegraph and the Signal corps were put in requisition to endeavor to prevent the escape of the assassins, and all the troops around Washington are under arms.

Popular report points to a somewhat celebrated actor of known secession proclivities as the assassin; but it would be unjust to name him until some further evidence of his guilt is obtained. It is rumored that the person alluded to is in custody.

The latest advices from Secretary Seward reveals more desperate work there than at first supposed. Seward's wounds are not in themselves fatal, but, in connection with his recent injuries, and the great loss of blood he has sustained, his recovery is questionable.

It was Clarence A. Seward, instead of William H. Seward, Jr., who was wounded. Fred Seward was also badly cut, as were also three nurses, who were in attendance upon the Secretary, showing that a desperate struggle took place there. The wounds of the whole party were dressed.

One o'clock A.M.

The President is perfectly senseless, and there is not the slightest hope of his surviving. Physicians believe that he will die before morning. All of his Cabinet except Secretary Seward, are with him. Speaker Colfax, Senator Farwell, of Maine, and many other gentlemen, are also at the house awaiting the termination.

The scene at the President's bedside is described by one who witnessed it as most affecting. He was surrounded by his Cabinet ministers, all of whom were bathed in tears, not even excepting Mr. Stanton, who, when informed by Surgeon General Barnes, that the President could not live until morning, exclaimed, "Oh, no, General; no—no;" and with an impulse, natural as it was unaffected, immediately sat down on a chair near his bedside and wept like a child.

Senator Sumner was seated on the right of the President's couch, near the head, holding the right hand of the President in his own. He was sobbing like a woman, with his head bowed down almost on the pillow of the bed on which the President was lying.

Two o'clock A.M.

The President is still alive, but there is no improvement in his condition.

* * *

Kennedy Killed by Sniper!

by Tom Wicker
(*The New York Times,* November 23, 1963)

KENNEDY IS KILLED BY SNIPER AS HE RIDES IN CAR IN DALLAS; JOHNSON SWORN IN ON PLANE.

Gov. Connally Shot; Mrs. Kennedy Safe.

President Is Struck Down by a Rifle Shot From Building on Motorcade Route— Johnson, Riding Behind, Is Unhurt.

DALLAS, Nov. 22—President John Fitzgerald Kennedy was shot and killed by an assassin today.

He died of a wound in the brain caused by a rifle bullet that was fired at him as he was riding through downtown Dallas in a motorcade.

Vice President Lyndon Baines Johnson, who was riding in the third car behind Mr. Kennedy's, was sworn in as the 36th President of the United States 99 minutes after Mr. Kennedy's death.

Mr. Johnson is 55 years old; Mr. Kennedy was 46.

Shortly after the assassination, Lee H. Oswald, who once defected to the Soviet Union and who has been active in the Fair Play for Cuba Committee, was arrested by the Dallas police. Tonight he was accused of the killing.

Suspect Captured After Scuffle

Oswald, 24 years old, was also accused of slaying a policeman who had approached him in the street. Oswald was subdued after a scuffle with a second policeman in a nearby theater.

President Kennedy was shot at 12:30 P.M., Central Standard Time (1:30 P.M., New York time). He was pronounced dead at 1 P.M. and Mr. Johnson was sworn in at 2:39 P.M.

Mr. Johnson, who was uninjured in the shooting, took his oath in the Presidential jet plane as it stood on the runway at Love Field. The body of Mr. Kennedy was aboard. Immediately after the oath-taking, the plane took off for Washington.

Standing beside the new President as Mr. Johnson took the oath of office was Mrs. John F. Kennedy. Her stockings were spattered with her husband's blood.

Gov. John B. Connally, Jr., of Texas, who was riding in the same car with Mr. Kennedy, was severely wounded in the chest, ribs and arm. His condition was serious, but not critical.

The killer fired the rifle from a building just off the motorcade route. Mr. Kennedy, Governor Connally and Mr. Johnson had just received an enthusiastic welcome from a large crowd in downtown Dallas.

Mr. Kennedy apparently was hit by the first of what witnesses believed were three shots. He was driven at high speed to Dallas Parkland Hospital. There, in an emergency operating room, with only physicians and nurses in attendance, he died without regaining consciousness.

Mrs. Kennedy, Mrs. Connally and a Secret Service agent were in the car with Mr. Kennedy and Governor Connally. Two Secret Service agents flanked the car. Other than Mr. Connally, none of this group was injured in the shooting. Mrs. Kennedy cried, "Oh no!" immediately after her husband was struck.

Mrs. Kennedy was in the hospital near her husband when he died, but not in the operating room. When the body was taken from the hospital in a bronze coffin about 2 P.M., Mrs. Kennedy walked beside it.

Her face was sorrowful. She looked steadily at the floor. She still wore the raspberry-colored suit in which she had greeted welcoming crowds in Fort Worth and Dallas. But she had taken off the matching pillbox hat she wore earlier in the day, and her dark hair was windblown and tangled. Her hand rested lightly on her husband's coffin as it was taken to a waiting hearse.

Mrs. Kennedy climbed in beside the coffin. Then the ambulance drove to Love Field, and Mr. Kennedy's body was placed aboard the Presidential jet. Mrs. Kennedy then attended the swearing-in ceremony for Mr. Johnson.

As Mr. Kennedy's body left Parkland Hospital, a few stunned persons stood outside. Nurses and doctors, whispering among themselves, looked from the window. A larger crowd that had gathered earlier, before it was known that the President was dead, had been dispersed by Secret Service men and policemen.

PRIESTS ADMINISTER LAST RITES

Two priests administered last rites to Mr. Kennedy, a Roman Catholic. They were the Very Rev. Oscar Huber, the pastor of Holy Trinity Church in Dallas, and the Rev. James Thompson.

Mr. Johnson was sworn in as President by Federal Judge Sarah T. Hughes of the Northern District of Texas. She was appointed to the judgeship by Mr. Kennedy in October, 1961.

The ceremony, delayed about five minutes for Mrs.

Kennedy's arrival, took place in the private Presidential cabin in the rear of the plane.

About 25 to 30 persons—members of the late President's staff, members of Congress who had been accompanying the President on a two-day tour of Texas cities and a few reporters—crowded into the little room.

No accurate listing of those present could be obtained. Mrs. Kennedy stood at the left of Mr. Johnson, her eyes and face showing the signs of weeping that had apparently shaken her since she left the hospital not long before.

Mrs. Johnson, wearing a beige dress, stood at her husband's right.

As Judge Hughes read the brief oath of office, her eyes, too, were red from weeping. Mr. Johnson's hands rested on a black, leatherbound Bible as Judge Hughes read and he repeated:

"I do solemnly swear that I will perform the duties of the President of the United States to the best of my ability and defend, protect and preserve the Constitution of the United States."

Those 34 words made Lyndon Baines Johnson, onetime farmboy and schoolteacher of Johnson City, the President.

Johnson Embraces Mrs. Kennedy

Mr. Johnson made no statement. He embraced Mrs. Kennedy and she held his hand for a long moment. He also embraced Mrs. Johnson and Mrs. Evelyn Lincoln, Mr. Kennedy's private secretary.

"O.K.," Mr. Johnson said. "Let's get this plane back to Washington."

At 2:46 P.M., seven minutes after he had become President, 106 minutes after Mr. Kennedy had become the fourth American President to succumb to an assassin's wounds, the white and red jet took off for Washington.

In the cabin when Mr. Johnson took the oath was Cecil Stoughton, an armed forces photographer assigned to the White House.

Mr. Kennedy's staff members appeared stunned and bewildered. Lawrence F. O'Brien, the Congressional liaison officer, and P. Kenneth O'Donnell, the appointment secretary, both long associates of Mr. Kennedy, showed evidences of weeping. None had anything to say.

Other staff members believed to be in the cabin for the swearing-in included David F. Powers, the White House receptionist; Miss Pamela Turnure, Mrs. Kennedy's press secretary; and Malcolm Kilduff, the assistant White House press secretary.

Mr. Kilduff announced the President's death, with choked voice and red-rimmed eyes, at about 1:36 P.M.

"President John F. Kennedy died at approximately 1 o'clock Central Standard Time today here in Dallas," Mr. Kilduff said at the hospital. "He died of a gunshot wound in the brain. I have no other details regarding the assassination of the President."

Mr. Kilduff also announced that Governor Connally had been hit by a bullet or bullets and that Mr. Johnson, who had not yet been sworn in, was safe in the protective custody of the Secret Service at an unannounced place, presumably the airplane at Love Field.

Mr. Kilduff indicated that the President had been shot once. Later medical reports raised the possibility that there had been two wounds. But the death was caused, as far as could be learned, by a massive wound in the brain.

Later in the afternoon, Dr. Malcolm Perry, an attending surgeon, and Dr. Kemp Clark, chief of neurosurgery at Parkland Hospital, gave more details.

Mr. Kennedy was hit by a bullet in the throat, just below the Adam's apple, they said. This wound had the appearance of a bullet's entry.

Mr. Kennedy also had a massive, gaping wound in the back and one on the right side of the head. However, the doctors said it was impossible to determine immediately whether the wounds had been caused by one bullet or two.

Back There

by Rod Serling

The Soothsayer cautions Caesar, "Beware the ides of March," but Caesar ignores his warning. Similarly, Corrigan, a time traveler in the following science fiction play, has foreknowledge of an assassination. Does Corrigan possess the power to change the course of history?

CHARACTERS

Corrigan, a young skeptic who learns better, and panics

William, an attendant; a calm gentleman who could be either a servant or a millionaire

Captain of Police, incorruptibly dense

Policeman, average

Wellington, tall and authoritative; cape and moustache

Police officer, young and sympathetic

Jackson, clubman

Millard, clubman

Whitaker, clubman

Attendant

Mrs. Landers, a fussy landlady

Lieutenant ⎫
           ⎬ two handsome young people
His girl ⎭

Landlady

Attendant Two

Two voices

Narrator

Act | **ONE**

Scene 1 *Exterior of club at night*

> *(Near a large front entrance of double doors is a name plaque in brass which reads "The Washington Club, Founded 1858." In the main hall of the building is a large paneled foyer with rooms leading off on either side. An attendant, William, carrying a tray of drinks, crosses the hall and enters one of the rooms. There are four men sitting around in the aftermath of a card game. Peter Corrigan is the youngest, then two middle-aged men named Whitaker and Millard, and Jackson, the oldest, a white-haired man in his sixties, who motions the tray from the attendant over to the table)*

Jackson. Just put it over here, William would you?

William. Yes, sir.

(He lays the tray down and walks away from the table)

Corrigan. Now what's your point? That if it were possible for a person to go back in time there'd be nothing in the world to prevent him from altering the course of history—is that it?

Millard. Let's say, Corrigan, that you go back in time. It's October, 1929. The day before the stock market crashed. You know on the following morning that the securities are going to tumble into an abyss. Now using that prior knowledge, there's a hundred things you can do to protect yourself.

Corrigan. But I'm an anachronism back there. I don't really belong back there.

Millard. You could sell out the day before the crash.

Corrigan. But what if I did and that started the crash earlier? Now history tells us that on October 24th, 1929, the bottom dropped out of the stock market. That's a fixed date. October 24th, 1929. It exists as an event in the history of our times. It *can't* be altered.

Millard. And I say it can. What's to prevent it? What's to prevent me, say, from going to a broker on the morning of October 23rd?

Corrigan. Gentlemen, I'm afraid I'll have to leave this time travel to H. G. Wells. I'm much too tired to get into any more metaphysics this evening. And since nobody has ever gone back in time, the whole blamed thing is much too theoretical. I'll probably see you over the weekend.

Whitaker. Don't get lost back in time now, Corrigan.

Corrigan. I certainly shall not. Good night, everybody.

Voices. Good night, Pete. Good night, Corrigan. See you tomorrow.

(Corrigan *walks out into the hall and heads toward the front door*)

William (*the attendant*). (*Going by*) Good night, Mr. Corrigan.

Corrigan. Good night, William. (*Then he looks at the elderly man a little more closely*) Everything all right with you, William? Looks like you've lost some weight.

William (*With a deference built of a forty-year habit pattern*). Just the usual worries, sir. The stars and my salary are fixed. It's the cost of living that goes up.

(Corrigan *smiles, reaches in his pocket, starts to hand him a bill*)

William. Oh no, sir, I couldn't.

Corrigan (*Forcing it into his hand*). Yes, you can, William. Bless you and say hello to your wife for me.

William. Thank you so much, sir. (*A pause*) Did you have a coat with you?

Corrigan. No. I'm rushing the season a little tonight, William. I felt spring in the air. Came out like this.

William (*Opening the door*). Well, April *is* spring, sir.

Corrigan. It's getting there. What is the date, William?

William. April 14th, sir.

Corrigan. April 14th. (*Then he turns, grins at the attendant*) 1965—right?

William. I beg your pardon, sir? Oh, yes, sir. 1965.

Corrigan (*Going out*). Good night, William. Take care of yourself. (*He goes out into the night*)

Scene 2 *Exterior of the club*

> (*The door closes behind Corrigan. He stands there near the front entrance. The light from the street light illuminates the steps. There's the sound of chimes from the distant steeple clock. Corrigan looks at his wrist watch, holding it out toward the light so it can be seen more clearly. Suddenly his face takes on a strange look. He shuts his eyes and rubs his temple. Then he looks down at his wrist again. This time the light has changed. It's a*

*wavery, moving light, different from what
it had been. Corrigan looks across toward
the light again. It's a gas light now. He
reacts in amazement. The chimes begin to
chime again, this time eight times. He
once again looks at the watch, but instead
of a wrist watch there is just a fringe of
lace protruding from a coat. There is no
wrist watch at all. He grabs his wrist,
pulling at the lace and coat. He's dressed
now in a nineteenth-century costume. He
looks down at himself, looks again toward
the gas light that flickers, and then slowly
backs down from the steps staring at the
building from which he's just come. The
plaque reads "Washington Club." He
jumps the steps two at a time, slams
against the front door, pounding on it.
After a long moment the door opens. An
attendant, half undressed, stands there
peering out into the darkness)*

Attendant. Who is it? What do you want?

Corrigan. I left something in there.

*(He starts to push his way in and the attendant partially
closes the door on him)*

Attendant. Now here you! The Club is closed this
evening.

Corrigan. The devil it is. I just left here a minute ago.

Attendant *(Peers at him)*. You did what? You drunk,
young man? That it? You're drunk, huh?

Corrigan. I am not drunk. I want to see Mr. Jackson or
Mr. Whitaker, or William. Let me talk to William.
Where is he now?

Attendant. Who?

Corrigan. William. What's the matter with you? Where

did *you* come from? (*Then he looks down at his clothes*) What's the idea of this? (*He looks up. The door has been shut. He pounds on it again, shouting*) Hey! Open up!

Voice (*From inside*). You best get away from here or I'll call the police. Go on. Get out of here.

(*Corrigan backs away from the door, goes down to the sidewalk, stands there, looks up at the gas light, then up and down the street, starts at the sound of noises. It's the clip-clop of horses' hooves and the rolling, squeaky sound of carriage wheels. He takes a few halting, running steps out into the street. He bites his lip, looks around*)

Corrigan (*Under his breath*). I'll go home. That's it. Go home. I'll go home. (*He turns and starts to walk and then run down the street, disappearing into the night*)

Scene 3 *Hallway of rooming house*

> (*There is the sound of a doorbell ringing. Mrs. Landers, the landlady, comes out from the dining room and goes toward the door*)

Mrs. Landers. All right. All right. Have a bit of patience. I'm coming.

Mrs. Landers (*Opening door*). Yes?

Corrigan. Is this 19 West 12th Street?

Mrs. Landers. That's right. Whom did you wish to see?

Corrigan. I'm just wondering if . . .

(*He stands there trying to look over her shoulder. Mrs. Landers turns to look behind her and then suspiciously back toward Corrigan*)

Mrs. Landers. Whom did you wish to see, young man?

Corrigan. I . . . I used to live here. It's the oldest building in this section of town.

Mrs. Landers (*Stares at him*). How's that?

Corrigan (*Wets his lips*). What I mean is . . . as I remember it . . . it was the oldest—

Mrs. Landers. Well now really, young man. I can't spend the whole evening standing here talking about silly things like which is the oldest building in the section. Now if there's nothing else—

Corrigan (*Blurting it out*). Do you have a room?

Mrs. Landers (*Opens the door just a little bit wider so that she can get a better look at him. She looks him up and down and appears satisfied*). I have a room for acceptable boarders. Do you come from around here?

Corrigan. Yes. Yes, I do.

Mrs. Landers. Army veteran?

Corrigan. Yes. Yes, as a matter of fact I am.

Mrs. Landers (*Looks at him again up and down*). Well, come in. I'll show you what I have.

(*She opens the door wider and* Corrigan *enters. She closes it behind him. She looks expectantly up toward his hat and* Corrigan *rather hurriedly and abruptly removes it. He grins, embarrassed*)

Corrigan. I'm not used to it.

Mrs. Landers. Used to what?

Corrigan (*Points to the hat in his hand*). The hat. I don't wear a hat very often.

Mrs. Landers (*Again gives him her inventory look, very unsure of him now*). May I inquire as to what your business is?

Corrigan. I'm an engineer.

Mrs. Landers. Really. A professional man. Hmmm. Well, come upstairs and I'll show you.

(*She points to the stairs that lead off the hall and* Corrigan *starts up as an army officer with a pretty girl comes down them*)

Mrs. Landers (*Smiling*). Off to the play?

Lieutenant. That's right, Mrs. Landers. Dinner at The Willard and then off to the play.

Mrs. Landers. Well, enjoy yourself. And applaud the President for me!

Lieutenant. We'll certainly do that.

Girl. Good night, Mrs. Landers.

Mrs. Landers. Good night, my dear. Have a good time. This way, Mr. Corrigan.

(*The lieutenant and* Corrigan *exchange a nod as they pass on the stairs. As they go up the steps,* Corrigan *suddenly stops and* Mrs. Landers *almost bangs into him*)

Mrs. Landers. Now what's the trouble?

Corrigan (*Whirling around*). What did you say?

Mrs. Landers. What did I say to whom? When?

Corrigan. To the lieutenant. To the officer. What did you just say to him?

(*The lieutenant has turned. The girl tries to lead him out, but he holds out his hand to stop her so that he can listen to the conversation from the steps*)

Corrigan. You just said something to him about the President.

Lieutenant (*Walking toward the foot of the steps*). She told me to applaud him. Where might your sympathies lie?

Mrs. Landers (*Suspiciously*). Yes, young man. Which army were you in?

Corrigan (*Wets his lips nervously*). The Army of the Republic, of course.

Lieutenant (*Nods, satisfied*). Then why make such a thing of applauding President Lincoln? That's his due, we figure.

Mrs. Landers. That and everything else, may the good Lord bless him.

Corrigan (*Takes a step down the stairs, staring at the lieutenant*). You're going to a play tonight?
(*The lieutenant nods*)

Girl (*At the door*). We may or we may not, depending on when my husband makes up his mind to get a carriage in time to have dinner and get to the theatre.

Corrigan. What theatre? What play?

Lieutenant. Ford's Theatre, of course.

Corrigan (*Looking off, his voice intense*). Ford's Theatre. Ford's Theatre.

Lieutenant. Are you all right? I mean do you feel all right?

Corrigan (*Whirls around to stare at him*). What's the name of the play?

Lieutenant (*Exchanges a look with his wife*). I beg your pardon?

Corrigan. The play. The one you're going to tonight at Ford's Theatre. What's the name of it?

Girl. It's called "Our American Cousin."

Corrigan (*Again looks off thoughtfully*). "Our American Cousin" and Lincoln's going to be there.

Corrigan (*Looks from one to the other, first toward the landlady on the steps, then down toward the soldier and his wife*). And it's April 14th, 1865, isn't it? Isn't it April 14th, 1865? (*He starts down the steps without waiting for an answer. The lieutenant stands in front of him*)

Lieutenant. Really, sir, I'd call your actions most strange.

(Corrigan *stares at him briefly as he goes by, then goes out the door, looking purposeful and intent*)

Scene 4 *Alley at night*

> (*On one side is the stage door with a sign over it reading "Ford's Theatre." Corrigan turns the corridor into the alley at a dead run. He stops directly under the light, looks left and right, then vaults over the railing and pounds on the stage door*)

Corrigan (*Shouting*). Hey! Hey, let me in! President Lincoln is going to be shot tonight!

(*He continues to pound on the door and shout*)

Act TWO

Scene 1 *Police station at night*

(It's a bare receiving room with a police captain at a desk. A long bench on one side of the room is occupied by sad miscreants awaiting disposition. There is a line of three or four men standing in front of the desk with several policemen in evidence. One holds onto Corrigan who has a bruise over his eye and his coat is quite disheveled. The police captain looks up to him from a list)

Captain. Now what's this one done? *(He peers up over his glasses and eyes Corrigan up and down)* Fancy Dan with too much money in his pockets, huh?

Corrigan. While you idiots are sitting here, you're going to lose a President!

(The captain looks inquiringly toward the policeman)

Policeman. That's what he's been yellin' all the way over to the station. And that's what the doorman at the Ford Theatre popped him on the head for. *(He nods toward Corrigan)* Tried to pound his way right through the stage door. Yellin' some kind of crazy things about President Lincoln goin' to get shot.

Corrigan. President Lincoln *will* be shot! Tonight. In the theatre. A man named Booth.

Captain. And how would you be knowin' this? I suppose you're clairvoyant or something. Some kind of seer or wizard or something.

Corrigan. I only know what I know. If I told you *how* I knew, you wouldn't believe me. Look, keep me here if you like. Lock me up.

Captain (*Motions toward a turnkey, points to cell block door*). Let him sleep it off.

(*The turnkey grabs Corrigan's arm and starts to lead him out of the room*)

Corrigan (*Shouting as he's led away*). Well you boobs better hear me out. Somebody better get to the President's box at the Ford Theatre. Either keep him out of there or put a cordon of men around him. A man named John Wilkes Booth is going to assassinate him tonight!

(*He's pushed through the door leading to the cell block. A tall man in cape and black moustache stands near the open door at the other side. He closes it behind him, takes a step into the room, then with a kind of very precise authority, he walks directly over to the captain's table, shoving a couple of people aside as he does so with a firm gentleness. When he reaches the captain's table he removes a card from his inside pocket, puts it on the table in front of the captain*)

Wellington. Wellington, Captain. Jonathan Wellington.

(*The captain looks at the card, peers at it over his glasses, then looks up toward the tall man in front of him. Obviously the man's manner and dress impresses him. His tone is respectful and quiet*)

Captain. What can I do for you, Mr. Wellington?

Wellington. That man you just had incarcerated. Mr. Corrigan I believe he said his name was.

Captain. Drunk, sir. That's probably what he is.

Wellington. Drunk or . . . (*He taps his head meaningfully*) Or perhaps, ill. I wonder if he could be remanded in my custody. He might well be a war veteran and I'd hate to see him placed in jail.

Captain. Well, that's real decent of you, Mr. Wellington. You say you want him remanded in *your* custody?

Wellington. Precisely. I'll be fully responsible for him. I think perhaps I might be able to help him.

Captain. All right, sir. If that's what you'd like. But I'd be careful of this one if I was you! There's a mighty bunch of crack-pots running the streets these days and many of them his like, and many of them dangerous too, sir. (*He turns toward turnkey*) Have Corrigan brought back out here. This gentleman's going to look after him. (*Then he turns to* Wellington) It's real decent of you sir. Real decent indeed.

Wellington. I'll be outside. Have him brought out to me if you would.

Captain. I will indeed, sir.

(Wellington *turns. He passes the various people who look at him and make room for him. His walk, his manner, his positiveness suggest a commanding figure and everyone reacts accordingly. The Captain once again busies himself with his list and is about to check in the next prisoner, when a young police officer alongside says:*)

Police Officer. Begging your pardon, Captain.

Captain. What is it?

Police Officer. About that Corrigan, sir.

Captain. What about him?

Police Officer. Wouldn't it be wise, sir, if—

Captain (*Impatiently*). If what?

Police Officer. He seemed so positive, sir. So sure. About the President, I mean.

Captain (*Slams on the desk with vast impatience*). What would you have us do? Send all available police to the Ford Theatre? And on what authority? On the word of some demented fool who probably left his mind someplace in Gettysburg. If I was you, mister, I'd be considerably more thoughtful at sizing up situations or you'll not advance one half grade the next twenty years. Now be good enough to stand aside and let me get on with my work.

Police Officer (*Very much deterred by all this, but pushed on by a gnawing sense of disquiet*). Captain, it wouldn't hurt.

Captain (*Interrupting with a roar*). It wouldn't hurt if what?

Police Officer. I was going to suggest, sir, that if perhaps we placed extra guards in the box with the President—

Captain. The President has all the guards he needs. He's got the whole Federal Army at his disposal and if they're satisfied with his security arrangements, then I am too and so should you. Next case!

(*The young police officer bites his lip and looks away, then stares across the room thoughtfully. The door opens and the turnkey leads* Corrigan *across the room and over to the door. He opens it and points out.* Corrigan *nods and walks outside. The door closes behind him. The young police officer looks briefly at the captain, then puts his cap on and starts out toward the door*)

Scene 2 *Lodging-house, Wellington's room*

> (*Wellington is pouring wine into two glasses. Corrigan sits in a chair, his face in his hands. He looks up at the proffered drink and takes it*)

Wellington. Take this. It'll make you feel better. (*Corrigan nods his thanks, takes a healthy swig of the wine, puts it down, then looks up at the other man*) Better?

Corrigan (*Studying the man*). Who are you anyway?

Wellington (*With a thin smile*). At the moment I'm your benefactor and apparently your only friend. I'm in the Government service, but as a young man in college I dabbled in medicine of a sort.

Corrigan. Medicine?

Wellington. Medicine of the mind.

Corrigan (*Smiles grimly*). Psychiatrist.

Wellington (*Turning to him*). I don't know the term.

Corrigan. What about the symptoms?

Wellington. They *do* interest me. This story you were telling about the President being assassinated.

Corrigan (*Quickly*). What time *is* it?

Wellington. There's time. (*Checks a pocket watch*) A quarter to eight. The play won't start for another half hour. What gave you the idea that the President would be assassinated?

Corrigan. I happen to know, that's all.

Wellington (*Again the thin smile*). You have a premonition?

Corrigan. I've got a devil of a lot more than a

premonition. Lincoln *will* be assassinated. (*Then quickly*) Unless somebody tries to prevent it.

Wellington. *I* shall try to prevent it. If you can convince me that you're neither drunk nor insane.

Corrigan (*On his feet*). If I told you what I was, you'd be convinced I was insane. So all I'm *going* to tell you is that I happen to know for a fact that a man named John Wilkes Booth will assassinate President Lincoln in his box at the Ford Theatre. I don't know what time it's going to happen . . . that's something I forgot—but—

Wellington (*Softly*). Something you forgot?

Corrigan (*Takes a step toward him*). Listen, please—(*He stops suddenly, and begins to waver. He reaches up to touch the bruise over his head*)

Wellington (*Takes out a handkerchief and hands it to* Corrigan). Here. That hasn't been treated properly. You'd best cover it.

Corrigan (*Very, very shaky, almost faint, takes the handkerchief, puts it to his head and sits back down weakly*). That's . . . that's odd. (*He looks up, still holding the handkerchief*)

Wellington. What is?

Corrigan. I'm so . . . I'm so faint all of a sudden. So weak. It's almost as if I were—

Wellington. As if you were what?

Corrigan (*With a weak smile*). As if I'd suddenly gotten drunk or some—(*He looks up, desperately trying to focus now as his vision starts to become clouded*) I've never . . . I've never felt like this before. I've never—(*His eyes turn to the wine glass on the table. As his eyes open wide, he struggles to his feet*) You . . . you devil! You drugged me, didn't you! (*He reaches out to grab* Wellington, *half struggling in the process*) You drugged me, didn't you!

Wellington. I was forced to, my young friend. You're a very sick man and a sick man doesn't belong in jail. He belongs in a comfortable accommodation where he can sleep and rest and regain his . . . (*He smiles a little apologetically*) his composure, his rationale. Rest, Mr. Corrigan. I'll be back soon.

(*He turns and starts toward the door.* Corrigan *starts to follow him, stumbles to his knees, supports himself on one hand, looks up as* Wellington *opens the door*)

Corrigan. Please . . . please, you've got to believe me. Lincoln's going to be shot tonight.

Wellington (*Smiling again*). And *that's* odd! Because . . . perhaps I'm beginning to believe you! Good night, Mr. Corrigan. Rest well. (*He turns and goes out of the room, closing the door behind him. We hear the sound of the key being inserted, the door locked*)

(Corrigan *tries desperately to rise and then weakly falls over on his side. He crawls toward the door. He scrabbles at it with a weak hand*)

Corrigan (*Almost in a whisper*). Please . . . please . . . somebody . . . let me out. I wasn't kidding . . . I know . . . *the President's going to be assassinated!* (*His arm, supporting him, gives out and he falls to his face, then in a last effort, he turns himself over so that he's lying on his back*)

(*There is a sound of a heavy knocking on the door. Then a* Landlady's *voice from outside*)

Landlady. There's no need to break it open, Officer. I've got an extra key. Now if you don't mind, stand aside.

(*There's the sound of the key inserted in the lock and the door opens. The young police officer from earlier is standing there with an angry-faced landlady behind him. The police officer gets down on his knees, props up* Corrigan's *head*)

Police Officer. Are you all right? What's happened?

Corrigan. What time is it? (*He grabs the officer, almost pulling him over*) You've got to tell me what time it is.

Police Officer. It's ten-thirty-five. Come on, Corrigan. You've got to tell me what you know about this. You may be a madman or a drunk or I don't know what—but you've got me convinced and I've been everywhere from the Mayor's office to the Police Commissioner's home trying to get a special guard for the President.

Corrigan. Then go yourself. Find out where he's sitting and get right up alongside of him. He'll be shot from behind. That's the way it happened. Shot from behind. And then the assassin jumps from the box to the stage and he runs out of the wings.

Police Officer (*Incredulous*). You're telling me this as if, as if it has already happened.

Corrigan. It *has* happened. It happened a hundred years ago and I've come back to see that it *doesn't* happen. (*Looking beyond the police officer*) Where's the man who brought me in here? Where's Wellington?

Landlady (*Peering into the room*). Wellington? There's no one here by that name.

Corrigan (*Waves a clenched fist at her. He still holds the handkerchief*). Don't tell me there's no one here by that name. He brought me in here. He lives in this room.

Landlady. There's no one here by that name.

Corrigan (*Holds the handkerchief close to his face, again waving his fist*). I tell you the man who brought me here was named—

(*He stops abruptly, suddenly caught by something he sees on the handkerchief. His eyes slowly turn to stare at it in his hand. On the border are the initials J.W.B.*)

Corrigan. J. W. B.?

Landlady. Of course! Mr. John Wilkes Booth who lives in this room and that's who brought you here.

Corrigan. He said his name was Wellington! And *that's* why he drugged me. (*He grabs the police officer again*) He gave me wine and he drugged me. He didn't want me to stop him. He's the one who's going to do it. Listen, you've got to get to that theatre. You've got to stop him. John Wilkes Booth! He's going to kill Lincoln. Look, get out of here now! Will you stop him? Will you—

(*He stops abruptly, his eyes look up. All three people turn to look toward the window. There's the sound of crowd noises building, suggestive of excitement, and then almost a collective wail, a mournful, universal chant that comes from the streets, and as the sound builds we suddenly hear intelligible words that are part of the mob noise*)

Voices. The President's been shot. President Lincoln's been assassinated. Lincoln is dying.

(*The landlady suddenly bursts into tears. The police officer rises to his feet, his face white*)

Police Officer. Oh my dear God! You were right. You *did* know. Oh . . . my . . . dear . . . God!

(*He turns almost trance-like and walks out of the room. The landlady follows him. Corrigan rises weakly and goes to the window, staring out at the night and listening to the sounds of a nation beginning its mourning. He closes his eyes and puts his head against the window pane and with fruitless, weakened smashes, hits the side of the window frame as he talks)*

Corrigan. I tried to tell you. I tried to warn you. Why didn't anybody listen? Why? Why didn't anyone listen to me?

(His fist beats a steady staccato on the window frame)

Scene 3 *The Washington Club at night*

> *(Corrigan is pounding on the front door of the Washington Club. Corrigan is standing there in modern dress once again. The door opens. An attendant we've not seen before appears)*

Attendant Two. Good evening, Mr. Corrigan. Did you forget something, sir?

(Corrigan walks past the attendant, through the big double doors that lead to the card room as in Act I. His three friends are in the middle of a discussion. The fourth man at the table, sitting in his seat, has his back to the camera)

Millard *(Looking up)*. Hello, Pete. Come on over and join tonight's bull session. It has to do with the best ways of amassing a fortune. What are your tried-and-true methods?

Corrigan *(His voice is intense and shaky)*. We were talking about time travel, about going back in time.

Jackson *(Dismissing it)*. Oh that's old stuff. We're on a new tack now. Money and the best ways to acquire it.

Corrigan. Listen . . . listen, I want to tell you something. This is true. If you go back into the past you can't change anything. (*He takes another step toward the table*) Understand? You can't change anything.

(*The men look at one another, disarmed by the intensity of Corrigan's tone*)

Jackson (*Rises, softly*). All right, old man, if you say so. (*Studying him intensely*) Are you all right?

Corrigan (*Closing his eyes for a moment*). Yes . . . yes, I'm all right.

Jackson. Then come on over and listen to a lot of palaver from self-made swindlers. William here has the best method.

Corrigan. William?

(*He sees the attendant from Act I but now meticulously dressed, a middle-aged millionaire obviously, with a totally different manner, who puts a cigarette in a holder with manicured hands in the manner of a man totally accustomed to wealth. William looks up and smiles*)

William. Oh yes. My method for achieving security is far the best. You simply inherit it. It comes to you in a beribboned box. I was telling the boys here, Corrigan. My great grandfather was on the police force here in Washington on the night of Lincoln's assassination. He went all over town trying to warn people that something might happen. (*He holds up his hands in a gesture*) How he figured it out, nobody seems to know. It's certainly not recorded any place. But because there was so much publicity, people never forgot him. He became a police chief, then a councilman, did some wheeling and dealing in land and became a millionaire.

What do you say we get back to our bridge, gentlemen?

(Jackson *takes the cards and starts to shuffle.* William *turns in his seat once again*)

William. How about it, Corrigan? Take a hand?

Corrigan. Thank you, William, no. I think I'll . . . I think I'll just go home.

(He *turns very slowly and starts toward the exit. Over his walk we hear the whispered, hushed murmurings of the men at the table*)

Voices. Looks peaked, doesn't he? Acting so strangely. I wonder what's the matter with him.

(Corrigan *walks into the hall and toward the front door*)

Narrator's Voice. Mr. Peter Corrigan, lately returned from a place "Back There"; a journey into time with highly questionable results. Proving, on one hand, that the threads of history are woven tightly and the skein of events cannot be undone; but, on the other hand, there are small fragments of tapestry that *can* be altered. Tonight's thesis, to be taken as you will, in The Twilight Zone!

For Malcolm, A Year After

by Etheridge Knight

*Antony is filled with grief and rage as he
stands over Caesar's corpse: "O, pardon me,
thou bleeding piece of earth, / That I am meek
and gentle with these butchers! / Thou art the
ruins of the noblest man / That ever lived in
the tide of times." In the following poem,
Etheridge Knight mourns the loss of Malcolm
X, the civil rights leader gunned down in 1965.*

Compose for Red a proper verse;
Adhere to foot and strict iamb,
Control the burst of angry words
Or they might boil and break the dam.
5 Or they might boil and overflow
And drench me, drown me, drive me mad.
So swear no oath, so shed no tear,
And sing no song blue Baptist sad.
Evoke no image, stir no flame,
10 And spin no yarn across the air.
Make empty anglo tea lace words—
Make them dead white and dry bone bare.

Compose a verse for Malcolm man,
And make it rime and make it prim.
15 The verse will die—as all men do—
But not the memory of him!
Death might come singing sweet like C,
Or knocking like the old folk say,
The moon and stars may pass away,
20 But not the anger of that day.

A Eulogy to Dr. Martin Luther King, Jr.

by Robert F. Kennedy

After Caesar's assassination Brutus and Antony speak to the public about the slain leader. Antony's fiery words incite a riot. After the assassination of Dr. Martin Luther King, Jr., on April 4, 1968, Senator Robert F. Kennedy delivered the following speech to an African-American audience. Senator Kennedy's underlying message, the opposite of Antony's, echoes Dr. King's philosophy of nonviolence. Three months later in California, Senator Kennedy also fell victim to an assassin's bullet.

I have bad news for you, for all of our fellow citizens, and people who love peace all over the world, and that is that Martin Luther King was shot and killed tonight.

Martin Luther King dedicated his life to love and to justice for his fellow human beings, and he died because of that effort.

In this difficult day, in this difficult time for the United States, it is perhaps well to ask what kind of a nation we are and what direction we want to move in. For those of you who are black—considering the evidence there evidently is that there were white people who were responsible—you can be filled with bitterness, with hatred, and a desire for revenge. We can move in that direction as a country, in great polarization—black people amongst black, white people amongst white, filled with hatred toward one another.

Or we can make an effort, as Martin Luther King did, to understand and to comprehend, and to replace that violence, that stain of bloodshed that has spread across our land, with an effort to understand with compassion and love.

For those of you who are black and are tempted to be filled with hatred and distrust at the injustice of such an act, against all white people, I can only say that I feel in my own heart the same kind of feeling. I had a member of my family killed, but he was killed by a white man. But we have to make an effort in the United States, we have to make an effort to understand, to go beyond these rather difficult times.

My favorite poet was Aeschylus. He wrote, "In our sleep, pain which cannot forget falls drop by drop upon the heart until, in our own despair, against our will, comes wisdom through the awful grace of God."

What we need in the United States is not division; what we need in the United States is not hatred; what we need in the United States is not violence or lawlessness but love and wisdom, and compassion toward one another, and a feeling of justice towards those who still suffer within our country, whether they be white or they be black.

So I shall ask you tonight to return home, to say a prayer for the family of Martin Luther King, that's true, but more importantly to say a prayer for our own country, which all of us love—a prayer for understanding and that compassion of which I spoke.

We can do well in this country. We will have difficult times. We've had difficult times in the past. We will have difficult times in the future. It is not the end of violence; it is not the end of lawlessness; it is not the end of disorder.

But the vast majority of white people and the vast majority of black people in this country want to live together, want to improve the quality of our life, and want justice for all human beings who abide in our land.

Let us dedicate ourselves to what the Greeks wrote so many years ago: to tame the savageness of man and to make gentle the life of this world.

Let us dedicate ourselves to that, and say a prayer for our country and for our people.

The Agony of Victory

by William Oscar Johnson

In ancient Rome mob violence was played out in the sports arena, as well as the political arena. For example, in 532 B.C., 30,000 Roman spectators were killed in riots at the chariot races, and in 59 B.C. riots broke out among fans at the Pompeii amphitheater during gladiator contests. The following article from Sports Illustrated *magazine looks at today's breed of rioting fans, who bear a striking resemblance to the Roman citizens in* Julius Caesar.

After three violent championship 'celebrations' in 1993, experts are pondering why people riot for the home team

On the evening of June 20 more than 5,000 Chicago police officers—four times the usual number for a Sunday night—were on duty in the streets at the moment John Paxson sank his three-pointer to clinch a third straight NBA crown for the Bulls. Armored trucks and prison vans were positioned to perform with maximum efficiency in handling mass arrests. The number of judges, prosecutors and public defenders on duty was doubled to expedite the processing of suspects. Extra firemen were at work. In all, the city spent $3 million to prepare for the postvictory violence that everyone knew was coming.

But no show of force could prevent the mayhem that burst over Chicago as the final buzzer sounded in far-off Phoenix. Over the next several hours thousands flooded into the streets. Dozens of shops were looted, and scores of cars were burned. A day-care center and four public schools were broken into. By dawn the rioting had claimed two lives, both random victims of celebratory bullets. Rosalind Slaughter, 26, was outside her South Side apartment building with her neighbors when she heard gunfire. Turning to go inside, Slaughter was three steps from her front door when she fell to the ground, a bullet in her temple. Slaughter's one-year-old daughter, one of her two children, was in her arms. Michael Lowery, 12, was sitting in front of his house in a middle-class South Side neighborhood when he was shot in the head. No arrests have been made in these murders, and none are expected.

After the madness was over, some Chicago officials proclaimed the riot of 1993 to have been tamer than that of '92; after all, there were only 682 arrests this time compared with 1,016 a year ago. Yet no one died in the '92 rioting, and some Chicagoans have suggested that this year's violence only seemed more benign because the fashionable Michigan Avenue shopping district was left largely undisturbed while inner-city neighborhoods bore the brunt of the ugly celebration.

Of the bullet that cut down her son, young Michael's mother, Patricia Lyles, said, "It could have happened anytime. It didn't have to be because of the Bulls. There is a lot of shooting that goes on around here."

True enough. But the Chicago violence was because of the Bulls' victory, and it thus took on a more frightening significance than if it had simply been part of the normal pattern of crime in the Windy City.

For what happened in Chicago had also happened in Montreal 11 days earlier, when the Canadiens won the Stanley Cup, and in Dallas four months before, after the Cowboys won the Super Bowl. Victory celebrations that turn violent are hardly new. But while there used to be an ugly scene every five or six years, then one every year, there have now been three in 1993.

These incidents are all evidence of a grim ritual in which we celebrate major sports triumphs by turning our cities' meanest streets even meaner, filling them with feral packs of kids and criminals who loot, shoot and leave their hometowns awash in blood, bullets and broken glass.

With large-scale violence now having occurred in two successive years, Chicago is beginning to rival Detroit when it comes to such mayhem. The Motor City was the scene of the first modern celebration riot in 1968 (after the Tigers won the World Series) and has since been plagued by rioting in '84 (the Tigers again) and in '89 and '90, after the Pistons won the NBA title. In the '84 night of violence, celebrants raped three women and shot to death a man who was in his car quietly awaiting a friend. That was the U.S.'s worst sports-victory melee—until the Pistons won their second NBA title, on June 14, 1990. On that night scores were injured by gunfire, stabbings and fights, and the death toll reached eight—including a four-year-old boy killed by a car; a man shot dead in a parking lot by a random bullet; and four people, three of them children, killed when a man drove his car onto a sidewalk and into a crowd of celebrants.

So what has caused this viciousness to replace ticker-tape parades as our way of celebrating big victories in sports? There have been many theories advanced over the years, some more original than others. For instance, after the Detroit mayhem of 1984, a New

York social psychologist, Carl Wiedemann, offered *Time* magazine his own list of explanations. Theory No. 1 had to do with the then rebounding auto industry. "Detroit is already making a comeback," Wiedemann said. "In sociological terms it is a perfect place for a revolution of rising expectations." Theory No. 2 suggested that the Tigers' rapid sweep of the San Diego Padres had left Detroit fans with "unspent warlike energy." And theory No. 3 speculated that the riots were "the equivalent of a rebellion by the Rustbelt against the Sunbelt."

Lieutenant Mike Hillman, an instructor at the Los Angeles Police Department's Unusual Occurrence Response Training Center, says of celebratory violence, "It's like the Wave. It starts, and if you don't do it, you screw up the whole thing, and people are going to taunt you and jeer at you. You do it because everyone else is doing it. If you're breaking windows and stealing and there is nobody there to do anything about it, you do it."

David Silber, chairman of the psychology department at George Washington University, says, "These kids live in cities that are virtual prisons of poverty. If a person is angry to begin with and is then exposed to a violent stimulus like a football, hockey or basketball game, that person is far more likely to act in a violent way. Adding alcohol to this mix makes it even more troublesome."

But the U.S. has always been a violent country, and our cities have always had impoverished areas. Why then has the triumph of the home team only recently provoked spasms of violence? "This is not 1950, when most people feared God and their parents and had respect for the police," says John Bryant, a community activist who is the director of Los Angeles's Operation Hope, a redevelopment group founded after that city's riots following the 1992

Rodney King verdict. "This is an era marked by weakened family structure, which means there is a lot less love by virtue of less discipline."

Each of this year's three victory riots was as different from the others as were the three cities in which they occurred.

The Dallas riot began as a massive midday civic celebration and parade on Tuesday, Feb. 9. The crowd was estimated as high as 400,000—far more than authorities had anticipated—and several city high schools reported absentee rates of more than 50% as young people from many neighborhoods thronged the downtown area. Most behaved themselves, but a few black youths, perhaps no more than 100, began harassing whites and Hispanics. They looted liquor stores, stripped vendors of Super Bowl memorabilia and did about $50,000 worth of damage to city buses, the same buses that had provided free rides to the parade site.

The Dallas violence was a day at the beach compared to the bloody street battles of Chicago or Detroit, but the city's conservative citizenry was shocked. The report of a task force that investigated the roots of the riot said the violence had "some racial overtones" and went on: "Post-parade disturbance, assaults and 'wilding' activities were generated by the combination of a sports-excitement atmosphere, the lack of sufficient police presence and mob psychology by groups—and therefore, by race."

Pettis Norman, a former Cowboy tight end who is now a Dallas businessman, and who was on the task force, says, "Dallas will win again soon, and next time the city will spend $3 million to have 10 times the police force out. We should be spending that three million trying to solve the problems that created the climate for such violence in the first place."

In Montreal on the night of June 9, the climate for

violence had nothing to do with race and little to do with sports. Nor was it spontaneous. More than half an hour before the Canadiens completed their Stanley Cup victory over the Los Angeles Kings, crowds of young men, virtually all of them white, began swarming out of the subway outside the Forum on St. Catherine Street "like rats out of a sewer," as one witness put it. Many were carrying bricks and steel bars. Some had plastic garbage bags around their waists, soon to be filled with loot. When the exultant spectators tried to emerge from the Forum after the final siren, they had trouble getting out of the building because of the swirling mobs outside. Some 600 police officers, as well as a specially trained riot squad, were poised nearby. But no orders came for the cops to go into action.

The crowds headed east toward downtown. Police inertia was an unexpected boon to the dozens of professional looters who used the celebration violence as a cover for some skillfully organized robbery: After shop windows were broken, trucks backed up to the stores and thieves loaded in merchandise. The rioters did an estimated $10 million in property damage and thefts before the police finally went into action about midnight.

The next day Montreal police chief Alain St. Germain offered a limp defense. "Right now, in the context of human rights and freedoms, we're walking on eggshells," he said. "Police must have sufficient cause to intervene. You have to remember there weren't only rioters in front of the Forum. There were people there simply to celebrate the victory of the Canadiens."

But as Tomas Gabor, a University of Ottawa criminologist, points out, "If police fail to stop criminal acts, there is no one to send the message that vandalism and looting is unacceptable."

In contrast to its genteel image. Montreal is all too familiar with mob violence. When the Canadiens won the Cup in 1986, a frenzy of violence and looting occurred that has since become known as the Gucci riot because the city's most fashionable stores were the hardest hit. Merchants that year were also outraged by police timidity—which some observers said was the unintended result of criticism that the police had endured after they were accused of excessive brutality during a political riot in '80.

Two weeks after this spring's violence in Montreal only two people had been arraigned on criminal charges. The bulk of the suspects will be charged with "mischievous behavior," which carries a maximum sentence of six months.

This slap-on-the-wrist justice is in sharp contrast to the way Chicago prosecutors have been handling their cases. As of last week 164 suspects in this year's violence had been charged with some form of burglary, a felony punishable by a prison term of three to seven years, although probation is possible. There has been discussion among lawyers on both sides as to whether sentences will be harder or softer in light of the fact that the crimes occurred amid the heady atmosphere of a championship triumph.

John Eannace, chief of the criminal prosecutions bureau in the Cook County state's attorney's office, says, "We will argue that a burglary on the night of the Bulls' win cries out for a more severe sentence. The victory is an aggravating factor. The motive behind these crimes is the destruction of property. They should be treated accordingly."

On the other hand, Shelton Green, chief of felony and trial for the Cook County public defender, says, "We would explain to the judge that the Bulls did something that has not happened in 20 years. Our client maybe had a couple. He was there. Look at the circumstances, Judge, we would say. It just happened in the moment, and the sentence should be minimal, definitely probation."

If what happened to culprits caught breaking the law in Chicago during the riot of 1992 is any indication, Cook County judges are going to be harsh. In all, 391 people were charged with felonies, and in the 281 cases concluded so far, 76 individuals were sent to prison for more than a year, two for less than a year, 161 were placed on probation, and 42 were found not guilty—results that are tougher than those in the general run of burglary cases.

But justice moves slowly in Chicago, and last week, as the city was still tallying the costs of the riot of 1993, the fates of four young men who had been arrested in the '92 melee were being decided in a Cook County courtroom. Three of the rioters—Gregory Jackson, Michael Howard and Lloyd Harwood—were ready to be sentenced by Circuit Judge Thomas Durkin following their convictions on charges of being among a mob that looted a grocery store. Durkin noted that the trio had helped cause $40,000 in damage and that they had thrown bottles and cans at the officers who had arrived to arrest them even as they were grabbing merchandise off the shelves. All three had no previous convictions, and Durkin sentenced each of them to 21 days in jail, two years of felony probation and 120 hours of community service, which means picking up trash and helping stranded motorists along Chicago's busy expressways.

The fourth young man appearing in Durkin's courtroom was Bertrand Davis, 22, who was in the second and final day of a jury trial on the charge that he had been one of a gang of eight or 10 males who had beaten and robbed three Koreans on the night in question.

According to prosecutors Tom Lyons and David

Styler, only one victim, Jong Kim, was willing to testify, but he offered a frightening account of what goes on during the wild hours of a championship celebration. According to Kim's testimony the gang, riding in three cars, cornered the auto of the victims, forcing them at gunpoint to pull into a side street. The gang demanded money. Kim and his friends refused, so the beating began, with punches, kicks and a beer bottle. They then turned over their cash—$38.

After that, the gang demanded the Bull T-shirts, emblazoned with the slogan REAL MEN WEAR RED, that all three victims were wearing, and the beating resumed until the T-shirts were surrendered. A man Kim identified as Davis then opened the victims' car trunk and found 33 more Bull T-shirts in a box, which he stole. The same man also found a windshield ice scraper and started beating Kim with it while demanding more money. By then Kim had suffered many cuts and a broken wrist.

The gang finally fled. The police found the shirtless, bleeding victims sitting in the street. Forty-five minutes later Kim spotted Davis crossing the street with another man and pointed him out to police as his assailant.

Davis insisted at his trial that he had been with his girlfriend when the assault took place and that he had just crossed the street to buy cigarettes when the police descended on him. The prosecution presented testimony that the arresting officers had found bloodstained money in Davis's pocket.

After four hours of deliberation the jury acquitted Davis. No one will be held accountable for the pain inflicted on Kim and his friends during a night of violence nearly forgotten after the passage of a year and yet another Bull victory riot.

With the World Series, the next championship milestone on the sporting calendar, less than four months away, is another ugly outburst of violence in 1993 inevitable? Not necessarily, pointed out the *Vancouver Sun* on June 15. Recalling those who celebrated the World Series victory of the Toronto Blue Jays last fall, the *Sun* remarked. "They were cool. Liquor bottles stayed in the bars. . . . When cops on horseback asked the revelers to move back onto the sidewalks, most obliged. It was a mixed crowd. Whites, blacks, Asians, mixing together, milling, hanging out, cheering."

The hope is that Toronto was not a quaint exception. The very real fear is that the events of Dallas, Montreal and Chicago are now the rule.

Wild in the Streets

When the Tigers swept the World Series in 1984, youths in Detroit attacked their hometown, a phenomenon that now has become depressingly common after sports triumphs in other cities.

Date	Event	The Human Toll	Crime/Damage	Location
6/20/93	Bulls win third title	Three dead, dozens injured, 700 arrested	Shootings, burglary, disorderly conduct; $150,000 (early estimate)	Chicago
4/9/93	Canadiens win Stanley Cup	168 injured, 115 arrested.	Stores destroyed, 47 police cars damaged, looting; $10 million.	Montreal
2/9/93	Cowboys win Super Bowl	26 injured, 25 arrested	Looting, fighting; $150,000	Dallas
6/14/92	Bulls win second title	100 injured, 1,000 arrested	Stores destroyed, 61 police cars damaged, looting, fires; $10 million	Chicago
6/14/90	Pistons win second title	Seven dead, hundreds injured, 140 arrested	Shootings, stabbings, fighting, looting, cars damaged	Detroit
5/24/86	Canadiens win Stanley Cup	Nine arrested	Looting, fighting, store windows smashed; $2 million	Montreal
1/20/85	49ers win Super Bowl	184 arrested	Store windows smashed, fires, rock and bottle throwing	San Francisco
10/14/84	Tigers win World Series	One dead, 20 injured, 41 arrested	Rapes, cars attacked, fires, rock and bottle throwing; $100,000	Detroit
10/18/77	Yankees win World Series	20 injured, 40 arrested	Yankee Stadium seats ripped out, turf torn up, vandalism	New York
10/17/71	Pirates win World Series	180 injured	Store windows smashed, fires, motorists attacked, armed robberies	Pittsburgh
10/10/68	Tigers win World Series	200 arrested	One rape, store windows smashed, fires	Detroit

The Tiger Who Would Be King

by James Thurber

Civil war follows Caesar's death and a new power struggle begins: Antony, Octavius, and Lepidus join forces against Brutus and Cassius. In the following fable, a similar power struggle occurs in the animal kingdom.

One morning the tiger woke up in the jungle and told his mate that he was king of beasts.

"Leo, the lion, is king of beasts," she said.

"We need a change," said the tiger. "The creatures are crying for a change."

The tigress listened but she could hear no crying, except that of her cubs.

"I'll be king of beasts by the time the moon rises," said the tiger. "It will be a yellow moon with black stripes, in my honor."

"Oh, sure," said the tigress as she went to look after her young, one of whom, a male, very like his father, had got an imaginary thorn in his paw.

The tiger prowled through the jungle till he came to the lion's den. "Come out," he roared, "and greet the king of beasts! The king is dead, long live the king!"

Inside the den, the lioness woke her mate. "The king is here to see you," she said.

"What king?" he inquired, sleepily.

"The king of beasts," she said.

"I am the king of beasts," roared Leo, and he charged out of the den to defend his crown against the pretender.

It was a terrible fight, and it lasted until the setting of the sun. All the animals of the jungle joined in, some taking the side of the tiger and others the side of the lion. Every creature from the aardvark to the zebra took part in the struggle to overthrow the lion or to repulse the tiger, and some did not know which they were fighting for, and some fought for both, and some fought whoever was nearest, and some fought for the sake of fighting.

"What are we fighting for?" someone asked the aardvark.

"The old order," said the aardvark.

"What are we dying for?" someone asked the zebra.

"The new order," said the zebra.

When the moon rose, fevered and gibbous, it shone upon a jungle in which nothing stirred except a macaw and a cockatoo, screaming in horror. All the beasts were dead except the tiger, and his days were numbered and his time was ticking away. He was monarch of all he surveyed, but it didn't seem to mean anything.

Moral: *You can't very well be king of beasts if there aren't any.*